Copyright © 2014 by Joe Anderson and Tim Nichols

All rights reserved
Printed in the United States of America
First Edition

No part of this book may be reproduced in any form or by any electronic or mechanical means, including information storage and retrieval systems, except for brief quotations in printed reviews, without the prior permission of the author.

Unless otherwise indicated, all Scripture quotations are taken from the New King James Version®. Copyright © 1982 by Thomas Nelson, Inc. Used by permission. All rights reserved.

Scripture quotations marked (NIV) are taken from the Holy Bible, New International Version®, NIV®. Copyright © 1973, 1978, 1984, 2011 by Biblica, Inc.™ Used by permission of Zondervan. All rights reserved worldwide. www.zondervan.com The "NIV" and "New International Version" are trademarks registered in the United States Patent and Trademark Office by Biblica, Inc.™

Author's translation or paraphrase indicated by an asterisk after the reference.

Cover illustration: *The Trial of Abraham's Faith* by Gustave Doré
Colorized and modified by William Britton

Table of Contents

Unit 1 Following Jesus the Priest **13**
    Lesson 1.1 Being a Disciple: The Sermon on the Mount 15
    Lesson 1.2 James (Overview and Introduction) 21
    Lesson 1.3 James (Quick to Hear) 25
    Lesson 1.4 James (Slow to Speak) 29
    Lesson 1.5 James (Slow to Anger) 35
    Lesson 1.6 Worldview Basics (Questions and Practice) 39
    Lesson 1.7 Worldview Basics (Story and Symbol) 43
    Lesson 1.8 Worldview Basics (Worship) 47
    Lesson 1.9 Signposts: Who's Your Daddy? 51
    Lesson 1.10 Spiritual Disciplines: The Lord's Prayer 57
    Lesson 1.11 Improvised Prayer 61
    Lesson 1.12 Praying for Others 65
    Lesson 1.13 Praying Thank You 69
    Lesson 1.14 The Prayer of the Tax Collector 73
    Lesson 1.15 Praying for Enemies and Those Who Have Hurt You 77

Unit 2 Following Jesus the King **81**
    Lesson 2.1 Royal Ethics: Children of Adam 83
    Lesson 2.2 Royal Ethics: Children of Abraham by Faith 89
    Lesson 2.3 Royal Ethics: Children of God in Christ 95
    Lesson 2.4 Royal Ethics: Formal Debate 99
    Lesson 2.5 Christian Worldview: Relating to Your Nation 107
    Lesson 2.6 Christian Worldview: Relating to Your Family 111
    Lesson 2.7 Christian Worldview: Relating to Your City 117
    Lesson 2.8 Christian Worldview: Relating to the Church 121
    Lesson 2.9 Christian Worldview: Relating to Your World 127
    Lesson 2.10 Christian Worldview: Your Vocation 131
    Lesson 2.11 Royal Disciplines: Praying in the Manner of the Lord's Prayer 135
    Lesson 2.12 Royal Disciplines: Praying the Psalms 141
    Lesson 2.13 Royal Disciplines: Basics of Being Great in the Kingdom of God 145
    Lesson 2.14 Royal Disciplines: Handling Conflict Well 149
    Lesson 2.15 Being a Good Friend 153

Lesson 2.16 Opposite Sex Friendships 157
Unit M Marriage and Sexuality **161**
   Lesson M-1 Sex in Marriage 161
   Lesson M-2 Why Wait? 165
   Lesson M-3 Pornography and Perversion 169
   Lesson M-4 Masturbation and Making Out 173
   Lesson M-5 Homosexuality 177
   Lesson M-6 Keeping Your Dignity 181
Unit 3 Following Jesus the Prophet **185**
   Lesson 3.1 God Does Supernatural Things 187
   Lesson 3.2 Hearing God Through Scripture 191
   Lesson 3.3 Hearing God Through His People 195
   Lesson 3.4 Hearing God Speak: Blessing 199
   Lesson 3.5 Hearing God Speak: Rebuke 203
   Lesson 3.6 Hearing God Speak: Comfort 207
   Lesson 3.7 Hearing God Speak: Questions and Answers 211
   Lesson 3.8 Responding in Faith 215
   Lesson 3.9 Devotional Apologetics Lesson 1: Start with God's Word 221
   Lesson 3.10 Devotional Apologetics Lesson 2: Without Excuse 225
   Lesson 3.11 Devotional Apologetics Lesson 3: Don't Get Robbed! 229
   Lesson 3.12 Devotional Apologetics Lesson 4: Answer a Fool 233
   Lesson 3.13 Devotional Apologetics Lesson 5: Loving the Different 237
   Lesson 3.14 Devotional Apologetics Lesson 6: Growing to Maturity 243
   Lesson 3.15 Devotional Apologetics Lesson 7: Living in Beauty 247
   Lesson 3.16 Is It Arrogant To Think We Have The Truth? 251
   Lesson 3.17 A Life Worth Sharing 255
   Lesson 3.18 The Triple-Triangle: Following Jesus as Priest, King and Prophet 261
End of Year Activities **266**

List of Illustrations

Illustration 1.1 *The Sermon on the Mount* (Gustave Doré, William Britton) ... 14
Illustration 1.2 *The Martyrdom of Stephen* (Gustave Doré, William Britton) ... 20
Illustration 1.3 *The Trial of Abraham's Faith* (Gustave Doré, William Britton) ... 24
Illustration 1.4 *Isaac Blessing Jacob* (Gustave Doré, William Britton) ... 28
Illustration 1.5 *The Death of Abel* (Gustave Doré, William Britton) ... 34
Illustration 1.7 *The Creation of Light* (Gustave Doré, William Britton) ... 42
Illustration 1.8 *The Last Supper* (Gustave Doré, William Britton) ... 46
Illustration 1.9a *The Formation of Eve* (Gustave Doré, William Britton) ... 50
Illustration 1.9b *Abram Journeying into the Land of Canaan* (Gustave Doré, William Britton) ... 53
Illustration 1.9c *The Ascension* (Gustave Doré, William Britton) ... 55
Illustration 1.10 *Jesus Praying in the Garden* (Gustave Doré, William Britton) ... 56
Illustration 1.11 *Jesus Walking on the Sea* (Gustave Doré, William Britton) ... 60
Illustration 1.12 *Jesus Healing the Demoniac* (Gustave Doré, William Britton) ... 64
Illustration 1.13 *The Annunciation to Mary* (Gustave Doré, William Britton) ... 68
Illustration 1.14 *The Pharisee and the Publican* (Gustave Doré, William Britton) ... 72
Illustration 1.15 *The Crown of Thorns* (Gustave Doré, William Britton) ... 76
Illustration 2.1 *The Creation of the Animals* (Gustave Doré, William Britton) ... 82
Illustration 2.2 *Abram Journeying into the Land of Canaan* (Gustave Doré, William Britton) ... 88
Illustration 2.3 *The Ascension* (Gustave Doré, William Britton) ... 94
Illustration 2.4 *The Disciples Plucking Grain on the Sabbath* (Gustave Doré, William Britton) ... 98
Illustration 2.5 *Christ and the Tribute Money* (Gustave Doré, William Britton) ... 106
Illustration 2.6 *Jesus and the Teachers in the Temple* (Gustave Doré, William Britton) ... 110
Illustration 2.7 *Jesus and the Woman of Samaria* (Gustave Doré, William Britton) ... 116
Illustration 2.8 *The Descent of the Holy Spirit* (Gustave Doré, William Britton) ... 120
Illustration 2.9 *Paul at Ephesus* (Gustave Doré, William Britton) ... 126
Illustration 2.10 *Cutting Down Cedars for the Temple* (Gustave Doré, William Britton) ... 130
Illustration 2.11 (1.10) *Jesus Praying in the Garden* (Gustave Doré, William Britton) ... 134
Illustration 2.12 (2.8) *The Descent of the Holy Spirit* (Gustave Doré, William Britton) ... 140
Illustration 2.13 *John the Baptist Preaching in the Wilderness* (Gustave Doré, William Britton) ... 144
Illustration 2.14 *The Meeting of Jacob and Esau* (Gustave Doré, William Britton) ... 148
Illustration 2.15 *Joseph Makes Himself Known to His Brothers* (Gustave Doré, William Britton) ... 152
Illustration 2.16 (2.7) *Jesus and the Woman of Samaria* (Gustave Doré, William Britton) ... 156
Illustration M-1 (1.9a) *The Formation of Eve* (Gustave Doré, William Britton) ... 160
Illustration M-2 *Boaz and Ruth* (Gustave Doré, William Britton) ... 164

Illustration M-3 *Joseph and Potiphar's Wife* (Guido Reni) 168
Illustration M-4 *The Creation of the Animals* (Gustave Doré, William Britton) 172
Illustration M-5 *Jesus and the Woman Caught in Adultery* (Gustave Doré, William Britton) 176
Illustration M-6 *Samson and Delilah* (Gustave Doré, William Britton) 180
Illustration 3.1 *The Walls of Jericho Falling Down* (Gustave Doré, William Britton) 186
Illustration 3.2 *The Temptation of Adam and Eve* (Gustave Doré, William Britton) 190
Illustration 3.3 *Moses Coming Down From Mt. Sinai* (Gustave Doré, William Britton) 194
Illustration 3.4 *Isaac Blessing Jacob* (Gustave Doré, William Britton) 198
Illustration 3.5 *The Serpent's Head Crushed* (Gustave Doré, William Britton) 202
Illustration 3.6 *Paul Shipwrecked* (Gustave Doré, William Britton) 206
Illustration 3.7 *Job and his Friends* (Gustave Doré, William Britton) 210
Illustration 3.8 *The Building of the Ark* (Gustave Doré, William Britton) 214
Illustration 3.10 *The Creation of Light* (Gustave Doré, William Britton) 224
Illustration 3.11 *The Temptation of Adam and Eve* (Gustave Doré, William Britton) 228
Illustration 3.12 *The Confusion of the Tongues* (Gustave Doré, William Britton) 232
Illustration 3.13 *Adam and Eve Driven out of the Garden* (Gustave Doré, William Britton) 236
Illustration 3.14 *The Death of Abel* (Gustave Doré, William Britton) 242
Illustration 3.15 *Peter and John at the Beautiful Gate* (Gustave Doré, William Britton) 246
Illustration 3.16 *Paul at Ephesus* (Gustave Doré, William Britton) 250
Illustration 3.17 *Christ Feeding the Multitude* (Gustave Doré, William Britton) 254

List of Figures

Figure 1.6 *A Well-Rounded Worldview* 38
Figure 3.9 *The Apologetics House* 220
Figure 3.18a *The Triple-Triangle* 260

UNIT 1: FOLLOWING JESUS THE PRIEST

Priesthood is about obedience. It is about hearing instructions well and following them to the letter. When God instituted the Levitical priesthood, He gave a mountain of regulations to the priests. He defined different kinds of sacrifices and what they were for. He gave instruction about which animals could be sacrificed and what sort of condition they had to be in. He regulated how long after the sacrifice the meat could be kept. Priests were required to exercise very little judgment; virtually everything about their jobs was already defined for them.

There are many things in the Christian life that are already defined for us—things that are simply a matter of obedience. Either we trust God enough to do them, or we do not. In this unit, we will embrace obedience to the basics of the Christian life. We will begin with the Sermon on the Mount, which was Jesus' teaching on what the life of a disciple should look like, and then we will continue into the book of James, which gives some further reflections on the life of discipleship. The commands contained in these Scriptures are not hard to understand; they are hard to live. We will need to embrace them as matters of obedience.

Because it is about obedience, priesthood is also about understanding the basics. We usually do not understand first; first we obey, and then slowly, learning by experience, we come to understand. As we seek to learn by experience, it is helpful to have some tools, some ways of thinking through our experience. To that end, we will introduce a basic set of worldview categories at this point in the curriculum.

The priesthood unit will conclude with an extended focus on prayer from a number of different angles. We will begin by learning how to use the Lord's Prayer as Jesus taught it to His disciples, then look at improvised prayer in the Scriptures. Students will learn to follow Christ as priests, interceding for the world before God in prayer, thanking God for all He has done, maintaining a humble attitude, and even praying for their enemies.

UNIT 1  **FOLLOWING JESUS THE PRIEST**

In the Sermon on the Mount, Jesus took the Old Testament commandments and pushed them "inside" (Matt 4:24-7:29).

LESSON 1.1

Being a Disciple: The Sermon on the Mount

UNIT 1

OVERVIEW

This year's curriculum is built around three different facets of our Christian life: priestly living, kingly living and prophetic living. The first part of the curriculum focuses on priestly living. Priests are called to obey God's commands without a lot of explanation because obedience changes the heart. The children of Israel were in their priestly period under Moses when God gave them the Law. Jesus is the new Moses and pushed the Law into the heart. The Sermon on the Mount is Jesus' explanation and fulfillment of the Law where He taught His disciples how to obey with the heart. In it, He took the Old Testament commands and pushed them "inside."

SOURCE MATERIAL

- Matthew 4:24-7:29

ACTIVITES

1. Interpret the Ten Commandments. Read Matthew 5:21-28. Jesus took two of the commandments and showed how they are about having a right heart. "You shall not murder" is not just about murder; it's also about hating your brother. A man who is lusting after a woman in his heart may not be committing adultery physically, but he's cheating on his wife in his heart. The command is about the heart, not just the external behavior. How could someone break the other eight commands in their heart without breaking them externally?

1. You shall have no other gods before Me. _____
_____
_____
_____
_____
_____
_____

Unit 1: Following Jesus the Priest

2. You shall not make any carved image...you shall not bow down to them, or serve them. _____
_____
_____
_____

3. You shall not take the name of the Lord your God in vain. _____
_____
_____
_____

4. Remember the Sabbath day, to keep it holy. _____
_____
_____
_____

5. Honor your father and mother. _____
_____
_____
_____

8. You shall not steal. _____
_____
_____
_____

9. You shall not bear false witness against your neighbor. _____
_____

Lesson 1.1

10. You shall not covet...anything that is your neighbor's.

2. Without Anyone Seeing: Doing Good and Journal Time. Think of something good you can do for someone, then do it. This could be something like giving to the poor or helping your elderly neighbor. The important thing for this activity is that you cannot tell anyone about your good deed; this activity is between you and the Lord. After doing your good deed, reflect on your experience in your journal or the space below.

Unit 1: Following Jesus the Priest

3. Without Anyone Seeing: Prayer and Journal Time. Using Matthew 6:5-13 as a model, pray to the Lord each day by yourself without telling anyone. Pray like this for a few days or more. You can pray the Lord's Prayer (Matt 6:9-13) and also pray for someone in need. Again, remember not to tell anyone about it. After practicing this type of prayer for a few days, reflect on your experience in your journal or the space below.

Lesson 1.1

EVALUTION

1. How does a priest relate to God? _____
_____
_____

2. What does obedience do to the disciple? _____
_____

3. What was Jesus doing in regard to the Old Testament Law in the Sermon on the Mount? _____
_____
_____

4. What Old Testament character does Jesus represent in the Sermon on the Mount? _____
_____
_____

5. Give one example of how Jesus pushed one of the Ten Commandments into the heart. _____
_____
_____

6. Why is it important to give money to the poor and to pray in secret? _____
_____
_____

After Stephen was stoned (Acts 7), persecution was a common experience for Christians. James wrote his letter to teach believers everywhere how to endure trial.

LESSON 1.2

James (Overview and Introduction)

UNIT 1

OVERVIEW

James was responsible for helping the Jerusalem church follow Jesus in the early days after the ascension. He wrote his letter after the stoning of Stephen and the initial persecution and scattering of the Jerusalem church that followed. Fittingly, he wrote on the subject of enduring in trial. The book of James begins with a 20-verse introduction, then divides from there into three main themes, each one considered in turn: swift to hear, slow to speak, and slow to wrath. In the introduction, James focuses on patient endurance, and how sin and righteousness happen in the believer's life.

SOURCE MATERIAL

- James 1:1-20
- Luke 4:1-13
- Genesis 3
- Habakkuk
- Job
- Psalm 49

ACTIVITES

1. Desire in Temptation.

Read James 1:12-18. According to James, what makes temptation work? _____
_____

Now go back and look at Jesus' temptation in Luke 4:1-13. What desire was the devil appealing to in each temptation?

Turning stones into bread: _____
_____

Bowing down to worship the devil: _____
_____

Unit 1: Following Jesus the Priest

Jumping off the pinnacle of the temple: _____

_____

Notice Luke 4:13. What do you think it means that "the devil had ended every temptation"? _____

_____

_____

_____

Now go all the way back to Genesis 3:6. What desire of Eve's was the devil appealing to? _____

_____

_____

_____

Compare your results for Jesus' and Eve's temptations to the categories in 1 John 2:15-17. Do the desires fit into John's categories? Explain your answer. _____

_____

_____

_____

2. Habakkuk and Job Comparison. Read the passages assigned to you by your teacher from the book of Job. Then read the book of Habakkuk (it's only three chapters long). In the space below, write a short essay comparing and contrasting Job's attitude with Habakkuk's. _____

_____

_____

_____

_____

_____

_____

_____

_____

_____

Lesson 1.2

EVALUATION

1. Who wrote the book of James? Which James? _____

2. To whom did he write the book? _____

3. What is the book about? _____

4. What makes it possible to be happy when life stinks? _____

5. What's so great about being mature? _____

6. What if I can't seem to be happy when my life stinks? _____

7. Where does temptation come from? _____

8. How does the desire family tree work? _____

9. How is the Christian life supposed to work instead? _____

10. What does it take to be the best of His creation? _____

God asked Abraham to offer his son Isaac, and Abraham was "quick to hear" and he obeyed God (Gen 22). Because of his obedience, he was called God's friend.

LESSON 1.3

James (Quick to Hear)

UNIT 1

OVERVIEW

In order to be the best of God's creation, even in bad circumstances, we must be quick to hear God. Quick to hear means more than just letting His words wash over us; we have to remember and obey, and that means loving our neighbors (including the poor) and showing mercy. If we sin by refusing to act on what we know, then our right knowledge doesn't profit the people who need help, and mere knowledge will not protect us from God's judgment. God will treat us the way we treat others; knowing better doesn't save us from God's judgment; *doing* better does.

SOURCE MATERIAL

- James 1:21-2:26
- Genesis 15:1-6, 22:1-19
- Psalm 41
- Proverbs 14:21

ACTIVITES

1. Doers of the Word. We don't want you to be "hearers only," but also doers of the word. Come up with something you can actually do to help people less fortunate than you are. Can you give away some of your clothes that you don't wear anymore? Give up snacks for a week and donate the money to the school's scholarship fund? What can you think of to do? Remember that at the heart of all charitable giving, it's just sharing. Here are some questions to think about.

What do I have more than enough of?_____
_____

Who has less than I do?_____
_____

What can I do this week to share?_____
_____

Unit 1: Following Jesus the Priest

What can I do this month?_____
_____

What can I do this year?_____
_____

2. Journal Time: Quick to Hear. In Activity 1, above, we challenged you to find something you could do to help those less fortunate than you. Reflect on what you learned by answering the following questions in your journal or the space below.

In helping those less fortunate than you, how were you being obedient to God?_____
_____
_____
_____
_____
_____
_____
_____
_____

Being "quick to hear" means not only hearing, but also obeying God's word. How were you "quick to hear" by helping others?_____
_____
_____
_____
_____
_____
_____
_____

Lesson 1.3

EVALUATION

1. What does James mean by "quick to hear"? _____
_____

2. If someone is just a hearer, but doesn't really do anything, what does James compare him to? _____
_____
_____

3. What are James' three tests to tell if you're really a doer? _____
_____
_____

4. What does James mean by taking care of the disadvantaged? _____
_____
_____
_____

5. Isn't being a good person and going to church enough? Why is it so serious if we kiss up to the rich people a little? I mean, after all, it's not like we're killing anyone! _____
_____
_____
_____
_____

Words matter. God chose Jacob, but Isaac wanted to bless Esau anyway. Isaac's plans were thwarted, and as a result, his sons became bitter enemies (Gen 27-28).

LESSON 1.4

James (Slow to Speak)

UNIT 1

OVERVIEW

God gave us good gifts, and He gave birth to us in order to make us the best of His creation. In order to grow into that calling, we will need to be slow to speak. It's easy to let our mouths get us into trouble, and we end up behaving exactly the opposite of our new nature as God's children. Because it's so easy for our mouths to run away, only a few of us should become teachers, and we should listen to the people with real wisdom: the ones who sow righteousness and make peace.

SOURCE MATERIAL

- James 3
- Psalm 148
- Proverbs 10:31

ACTIVITES

1. Blessing Activity. In biblical times, there were special moments of blessing where people took the time to say something good about another person. In Christianity today, we seem to have lost this ability. Today, you're going to get some practice. In the chart on the following pages, write your classmates' names down the left side. On the right side, briefly write something good about each person. Be specific.

Unit 1: Following Jesus as Priest

Name	A good thing you see in this person

Lesson 1.4

Name	A good thing you see in this person

Unit 1: Following Jesus as Priest

2. Journal Time: Slow to Speak. Think of a time recently when you "cursed" someone. This could be talking back to your parents, making a rude comment to a peer, gossiping about someone, or many other things. Answer the following in your journal or the space below.

Briefly write down how you recently "cursed" someone. _____
_____
_____
_____

Now write a prayer to God in your journal, confessing this sin. _____
_____
_____
_____
_____

If you feel God prompting you to, confess your sin to the person you "cursed."

3. Psalm 148. Read or sing Psalm 148 and write a prayer of response in the space below. _____
_____
_____
_____
_____
_____
_____
_____
_____
_____
_____
_____

Lesson 1.4

EVALUATION

1. Why should we be slow to speak?_____
_____

2. What does James compare the tongue to?_____
_____
_____
_____

3. Can the tongue be tamed? _____
_____

4. What unnatural combination of things does James say the tongue does? _____
_____

5. Why is it unnatural to say bad things about other people, especially since it seems to come so easily to us? _____
_____

6. Why shouldn't many people be teachers?_____
_____

7. To whom should we listen?_____
_____

8. How can we tell if a person is wise? _____
_____
_____

Cain never really learned this: wars and fights come from desires for pleasure that war in our members (Gen 4, Jas 4:1).

LESSON 1.5

James (Slow to Anger)

UNIT 1

OVERVIEW

The Father gave birth to us in order for us to be the best of His creation, but in order to grow into that calling, we need to be slow to anger. Fights among us come from our own lusts and pride; that same combination leads us into passing judgment on our brothers, making plans that ignore God, and defrauding our brothers. By contrast, if we will be patient and humble in our circumstances, God will be kind to us and give us what we need.

SOURCE MATERIAL

- James 4-5
- Psalm 145
- Proverbs 16:32

ACTIVITES

1. Class Discussion and Journal Time: Desires. Think about the following questions and be prepared to discuss them in class.

How do you submit a desire to God? Practically, what do you do?

But what does it mean to give a desire to God in prayer?

Unit 1: Following Jesus the Priest

But then what? Unless God removes the desire (which He sometimes does), you still have the desire, and now you're suffering because it's not being gratified. How can we deal with desires that we've committed to God and asked Him to meet, but He hasn't met yet, and the desires haven't gone away?

_____
_____
_____

After discussing these questions as a class, spend some time writing in your journal or the space below, considering the following questions.

What is a desire you have right now or have had in the recent past? _____
_____
_____

Has God given you what you desire, taken away the desire, or has He not met that desire yet?_____
_____

If God has already given you this desire, write a prayer thanking Him for His good gift. If He has taken away this desire, write a prayer, thanking Him for taking care of you and for giving you what is best for you. If you still have the desire, but God hasn't given you your desire, write a prayer, submitting your desire to God. Recognize in your prayer that it is a trial to have unmet desires, but, like all trials, this trial can lead to patience and maturity (Jas 1:2-4)._____
_____
_____
_____
_____

2. What Causes Fights? Think back to a disagreement, argument or fight that you were involved in sometime in the last week.

Write down a little about the situation._____
_____
_____
_____

Lesson 1.5

What was at the root of the conflict? _____

_____

_____

_____

_____

James says our conflicts come from our desires for pleasure. Would you say that's true in this case? Why or why not? _____

_____

EVALUATION

1. Where do fights come from? _____

_____

2. How does God respond to pride? _____

    How does He respond to humility? _____

3. What is the problem with speaking badly of someone else? _____

_____

_____

_____

4. What is the problem with making plans apart from God? _____

_____

5. What is the problem with getting wealthy through fraud? _____

_____

_____

6. In one word, how should we live? _____

    Whose example can we follow for patient living? _____

_____

A Well-Rounded Worldview

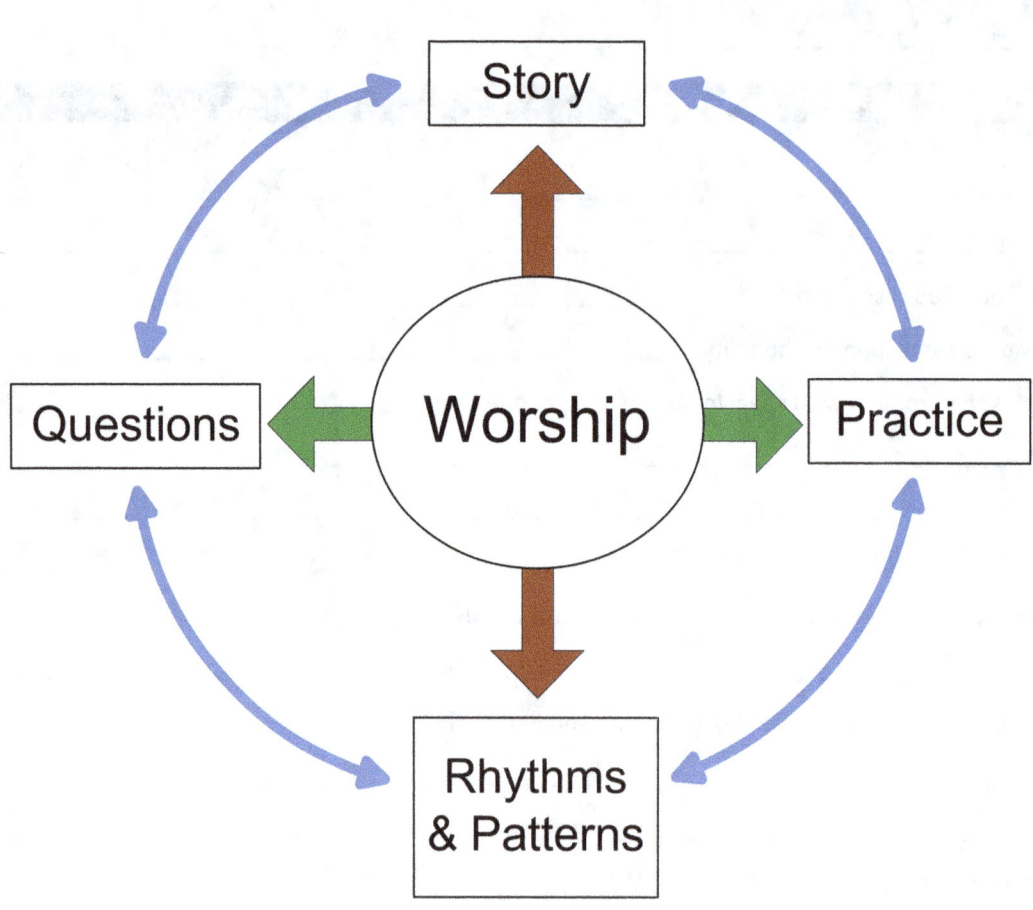

LESSON 1.6

Worldview Basics (Questions and Practice)

UNIT 1

OVERVIEW

Understanding worldviews and how they work requires mastering some basic conceptual tools. The next three lessons will introduce students to one such tool, made up of five components. This lesson teaches the first two components: Questions and Practice. The first component, Questions, is the way a worldview answers the questions about reality: What is God like? What is man? How should we live? etc. Practice is the way those answers are put into practice in everyday life.

SOURCE MATERIAL

- The book or movie trailer for *Notes from the Tilt-a-Whirl*, available online

ACTIVITES

1. What is Worldview? Lots of people talk about "worldview" these days. What do you think the word means? _____

_____

_____

_____

_____

_____

What would be some examples of different worldviews? _____

_____

_____

_____

_____

_____

Unit 1: Following Jesus the Priest

Think about the term "worldview." Why "worldview" instead of "worldsmell" or "worldtaste" or some other sense? _____

_____

2. *Notes from the Tilt-A-Whirl* Trailer Activity. After watching the trailer from N. D. Wilson's *Notes from the Tilt-a-Whirl*, list all the questions you can think of that were raised in the course of that two-minute clip. _____

_____

_____

_____

_____

3. Green Axis Activity. The Green Axis is about issues: what are the right answers, and are you actually living them out in your life? _____

_____

_____

_____

_____

_____

Read James 1:22. What James is calling for here is integrity across the Green Axis. Re-read James 1:21-2:26 with this in mind. What answers to the questions is James assuming? What items does he insist must be present in his readers' practice to really live out those answers? _____

_____

_____

_____

_____

_____

Now consider those same ethical issues that James raises from the standpoint (story) of naturalistic atheism. Does it make sense to control your mouth, in that story? Does it make sense to take care of weak and marginal people that no one cares about? What about keeping yourself unstained by the world? _____

_____

_____

_____

4. Doers of the Word Revisited. In Lesson 1.3 we challenged you to find a way to help people less fortunate than you. How are you doing? Have you had any more ideas? Are you executing these ideas?_____

_____

_____

_____

_____

EVALUATION

1. Define the terms Questions and Practice. _____

_____

_____

2. Do we always have harmony between the way we answer the Questions and our Practice? _____

_____

_____

3. What is an inevitable question?_____

_____

_____

4. What are some examples of inevitable questions? _____

_____

_____

Your worldview is driven by the story you believe you are living in. The Bible teaches that our Story started with a good creation by a good God (Gen 1).

LESSON 1.7

Worldview Basics (Story and Symbol)

UNIT 1

OVERVIEW

Stories are powerful, and the most powerful story of all is the one we think we're living in. That story (or those stories, if we're living by competing stories) dictates the choices we make, by inspiring us to be loyal to certain people and a certain picture of The Good Life. In turn, we constantly express and reinforce the story we think we live in by the symbols that we choose to surround ourselves with. Other people (especially advertisers) try to hijack our loyalties by surrounding us with different symbols that point to the story they want us to live by.

SOURCE MATERIAL

- Various commercials, including the Walmart/Coke "Stock up on Joy" Christmas commercial, available on Vimeo or YouTube
- Video clip from *Notes from the Tilt-A-Whirl*, chapter five: "Breathing Characters", available online

ACTIVITES

1. Symbol Hunt. Think through an average day, morning to night, and think of all the symbols or symbolic acts you encounter in an average day. Write these down in the space below. If you have time, take your workbook with you throughout your day today. Every time you see a symbol or a symbolic act, write it down. _____

_____
_____
_____
_____
_____
_____
_____
_____

Unit 1: Following Jesus the Priest

What's the big story (or stories) that all these symbols point back to? _____
_____
_____
_____
_____

2. Commercial Analysis. After watching the commercial(s) your teacher showed you in class, answer the following questions.

What's the picture of The Good Life that the commercial is trying to give you? _____
_____
_____
_____
_____

What's the story they're trying to sell you so that you will buy their stuff? _____
_____
_____
_____

Think of a commercial or advertisement you've seen. What picture of The Good Life is that commercial trying to give you? What story is the commercial trying to sell you so that you will buy their stuff? _____
_____
_____
_____
_____

EVALUATION

1. Define Story. _____
_____

2. What are some examples of a big story? _____
_____

3. How do fictional stories relate to the big story?_____
_____
_____

4. Choose a specific fictional story and explain how it points out an aspect of the big story._____
_____
_____
_____

5. What are the big issues on the Red Axis?_____
_____
_____

6. List three symbols that you see in a typical day, and explain how they point to a bigger story. ____
_____
_____

The Lord's supper is a symbol of unity. When we eat with one another, we see the world as it truly is.

LESSON 1.8

Worldview Basics (Worship)

UNIT 1

OVERVIEW

Worship is the world in microcosm. Everything in the world is in our worship in seed form, and everything in our worship finds its way out into the way we live in the world, often in ways we don't recognize.

SOURCE MATERIAL

- 1 Corinthians 11:17-34

ACTIVITES

1. Journal Time: Growing Seeds. Write about a time in your life when someone said or did something that changed your life for the better. What fruit has happened in your life because of the seed that person planted? How would life be different for you if that seed had never been planted? _____

_____
_____
_____
_____
_____
_____
_____
_____
_____
_____
_____
_____

Unit 1: Following Jesus the Priest

2. A Roman-ish Meal. Following your classroom activity, answer the following questions. Be prepared to discuss your answers in class.

How did it make you feel to be part of the Roman dining experience? _____
_____
_____
_____
_____

Would you be willing to eat like that every day? _____
_____
_____
_____
_____
_____
_____
_____

Why do you think we don't do that anymore? _____
_____
_____
_____
_____
_____
_____
_____
_____
_____

EVALUATION

1. How does worship relate to worldview? _____
_____
_____

2. Did Roman families all eat at the same time the way we do today? _____
_____
_____
_____

3. Even among the men, did they all eat the same food? _____
_____
_____
_____

4. Paul believed and taught that all of us are equal before God (Gal 3:28). So of course he tried to change the way they treated each other as unequal at the dinner table, right? _____
_____
_____

5. What did Paul do? _____
_____
_____

6. What was the effect of the early Church observing the Lord's table in the way Paul taught them? ___
_____
_____

7. So does worship change worldview? _____
_____
_____
_____

We are children of Adam who are called to be rulers over the earth.

LESSON 1.9

Signposts: Who's Your Daddy?

UNIT 1

OVERVIEW

Every Christian is a child of Adam by birth, a child of Abraham by faith, and a child of God in Christ. This lesson explores the ethical implications of living as the scion of this triple lineage: a child of Adam must cultivate and guard the creation; a child of Abraham must be a blessing; a child of God in Christ must make disciples.

SOURCE MATERIAL

- Genesis 1:28-30, 2:15, 9:1-7
- Genesis 12:1-3, Galatians 3:7-9
- John 1:12, Matthew 28:18-20

ACTIVITES

1. Blessings Brainstorm. Take some time to think through the blessings that you encounter on a daily basis. List one blessing from your heritage through Adam, one through Abraham, and one through God Himself for each part of your day.

From the time you wake up until you arrive at school:

Adam:_____

_____

Abraham:_____

_____

God:_____

_____

During your school day:

Adam:_____

_____

Unit 1: Following Jesus the Priest

Abraham: _____

_____

God: _____

_____

From after school to bedtime:

Adam: _____

_____

Abraham: _____

_____

God: _____

_____

2. Thanksgiving Prayer. In your journal or the space below, compose a prayer giving thanks to God for the blessings in your life. Be specific. _____

_____
_____
_____
_____
_____
_____
_____
_____
_____
_____
_____
_____
_____

We are children of Abraham by faith, blessed along with him and called to believe like he did.

Unit 1: Following Jesus the Priest

EVALUATION

1. What were Adam and Eve made to be? _____

2. Did Adam and Eve cease to be God's image at the fall? How do we know? _____
_____

3. What do we get because we're descendants of Adam and Eve? _____
_____

4. What is our responsibility as descendants of Adam and Eve? _____
_____

5. How do you think we're doing at our responsibilities as Adam's children? _____
_____
_____

6. What are our blessings as children of Abraham by faith? _____
_____

7. What are our responsibilities as children of Abraham by faith? _____
_____

8. How are we doing at our responsibilities as Abraham's children? _____
_____
_____

9. What are our blessings as children of God in Christ? _____
_____
_____

10. What are our responsibilities as children of God in Christ? _____
_____
_____

11. How do you think we are doing at our responsibilities as children of God in Christ? __
_____
_____

We are children of God in Christ, commissioned and blessed to carry out His mission on earth.

Jesus is our model of prayer.

LESSON 1.10

Spiritual Disciplines: The Lord's Prayer

UNIT 1

OVERVIEW

The first of the spiritual disciplines is prayer. The Lord's Prayer is the model Christ gave us for all other prayer. As priests, we are compelled to start our prayer journey by praying the Lord's Prayer regularly, word for word, as Jesus commanded: "When you pray say... [The Lord's Prayer]" (Luke 11:2).

SOURCE MATERIAL

- Luke 11:1-4
- Matthew 6:9-13

ACTIVITES

1. Word Association: The Lord's Prayer. Write down the first words or phrases that come to your mind when you hear someone say, "The Lord's Prayer." You can also write short sentences that come to mind, but you should avoid paragraph answers. _____

_____

_____

_____

_____

2. Pray It. For the next seven days, pray the Lord's Prayer once a day with some specific subject or situation in mind. On the sheet below or in your journal, make a note of what you prayed about and any additional thoughts that occur to you.

Day 1: When?_____

What did you pray about?_____

Additional thoughts?_____

Day 2: When?_____

Unit 1: Following Jesus the Priest

What did you pray about? _____

Additional thoughts? _____

Day 3: When? _____

What did you pray about? _____

Additional thoughts? _____

Day 4: When? _____

What did you pray about? _____

Additional thoughts? _____

Day 5: When? _____

What did you pray about? _____

Additional thoughts? _____

Day 6: When? _____

What did you pray about? _____

Additional thoughts? _____

Day 7: When? _____

What did you pray about? _____

Additional thoughts? _____

3. Journal Time: The Lord's Prayer. Write any new insights you have after having prayed the Lord's Prayer for a few days. _____

_____

_____

_____

_____

_____

_____

_____

Lesson 1.10

EVALUATION

1. Did Jesus give the Lord's Prayer as a model or as a rote prayer to be prayed word-for-word? _____
_____
_____

2. How does the Lord's Prayer teach us to relate to God? _____

3. Why do you think the Lord's Prayer starts with praise? _____
_____
_____

4. What does "Thy kingdom come, Thy will be done, on earth as it is in heaven" mean? _____
_____
_____
_____

5. Is the request for bread really just talking about bread? _____
_____
_____

6. Why are we to pray that God would forgive us *as we forgive others*? _____
_____
_____

7. We are to pray that God would "Lead us not into temptation." Would God ever lead us into temptation? _____

    Then what does this mean? _____
_____

8. When the Lord's Prayer says, "deliver us from evil," what kind of evil is it referring to? _____
_____
_____
_____

When Peter stepped out of the boat in faith and then faltered, Jesus was still faithful to answer his prayer (Matt 14:22-33).

LESSON 1.11

Improvised Prayer

UNIT 1

OVERVIEW

The Scriptures give us the wording for many prayers that we can and should pray (e.g., the Lord's Prayer and many of the psalms), but they also teach us to simply *talk* to God. In order to maintain biblical balance following our lesson on praying the Lord's Prayer word-for-word, this lesson will focus on praying in our own words (especially in emergencies!), using Peter as an example.

SOURCE MATERIAL

- Matthew 14:22-33
- Psalm 13

ACTIVITES

1. Journal Time: Praying for Real. If you could take just one situation or request to God, without any fear of judgment, what would it be? What would you want to say to God?

Unit 1: Following Jesus the Priest

Take a few minutes to write out a prayer on your chosen subject here or in your journal. Tell God what's really in your heart._____

_____

_____

_____

_____

Now take the time to pray through the Lord's Prayer on your chosen subject. Do your best to relate each phrase in the prayer to something about your situation.

2. Sing Psalm 13. Below are the words of Psalm 13 from Sing Psalms.

How long will you forget me, Lord?
Will you forget always?
How long, Lord, will you hide your face
And turn from me your gaze?

How long must I be sad each day
In deep perplexity?
How long will my opponent stand
In triumph over me?

O Lord my God, consider me
And give me your reply.
Light up my eyes or I will sleep
The sleep of those who die.

Then would my enemy declare,
"At last I've laid him low!"
And so my foes would sing for joy
To see my overthrow.

But still I trust your constant love;
You save and set me free.
With joy I will extol the Lord
Who has been good to me.

Lesson 1.11

EVALUATION

1. What was Peter's heart like when he asked Jesus to save him from drowning? _____
_____
_____

2. How did Jesus respond to his request? _____
_____

3. Do you need to make sure your heart is right before you ask God for something? _____
_____
_____
_____
_____

4. Can you say something to God that isn't true? _____
_____
_____
. _____

The disciples thought they could cast out a demon without bothering God; Jesus told them that they needed to pray for the demon-possessed man (Matt 17:14-21).

LESSON 1.12

Praying for Others

UNIT 1

OVERVIEW

Having learned to pray for their own needs and concerns honestly, students need to also pray for others. This is an application of the Lord's Prayer, as well as of the golden rule.

SOURCE MATERIAL

- Luke 11:1-4
- Matthew 7:12

ACTIVITES

1. Praying God's Will. Although we often don't exactly know God's will for a situation, much of the time we do know at least some of what God wants to happen. For example, He wants marriages to succeed, He wants people to be kind to each other, He wants justice and mercy.

List out some situations you know of where God's will is not being done right now. _____

_____

_____

_____

_____

_____

Pick one of these situations and identify something that you know is God's will for the situation. _____

_____

_____

_____

_____

Unit 1: Following Jesus the Priest

Pray God's will for the situation; write out your prayer in the space below or in your journal. _____
_____
_____
_____
_____
_____

2. Golden Rule Prayer. Much of the time God makes His will clear to us, but sometimes we just don't know His will for a specific situation. Repeat the above activity, but this time with a situation where you might have a guess or two about God's will, but nobody really knows for sure.

Write down some situations where you need guidance or you have a need or desire, but you're not sure what God's will for the situation is. _____
_____
_____
_____
_____

Pick one of these situations and write down why you are not sure what God's will in it is. _____
_____
_____
_____
_____

Use the Golden Rule as you pray for this situation (pray for others as you would have them pray for you). Write out your prayer in the space below or in your journal. _____
_____
_____
_____
_____
_____

EVALUATION

1. What does the Lord's Prayer teach us to pray for earthly situations? _____
_____
_____

2. Do we ever really know what God's will is? _____
_____
_____

3. What are some examples of situations where we know God's will? _____
_____
_____
_____
_____

4. Do we know God's will in every situation? _____
_____
_____

5. What are some examples of situations where we don't know God's will? _____
_____
_____
_____
_____
_____

6. How should we pray in a situation where we don't know God's will? _____
_____
_____
_____
_____

When Mary was told that she would bring forth a child who would be the Savior of the world, she responded with a prayer of gratitude (Luke 1:46-55).

LESSON 1.13

Praying Thank You

UNIT 1

OVERVIEW

If we pray the Lord's Prayer, and we pray honestly for our own and others' needs, then we will be seeing answers to prayer. When God answers, we need to celebrate—and we need to include Him in the celebration. This means praying prayers of thanksgiving, including thanksgiving for the things we didn't think to ask for.

SOURCE MATERIAL

- Luke 17:11-19
- Psalms 104, 107, 148

ACTIVITES

1. Answered Prayer. We've been focusing on prayer for a while now. Take a few minutes to recall the things you've prayed for. Make a list below.

How has God answered your prayers so far?

2. Psalm Writing. A number of psalms praise God for various aspects of His character and works. Just like with answered prayer, we often feel like we have nothing to be thankful for, just because we never bothered to notice what's going on. In the space below or in your journal, write a praise psalm of your own. Here are a couple of "tools" you can use:

- **Parallelism:** Most of the psalms are written in couplets, where the first line says something, and then the second line responds to the first in some way—either saying the same thing in a different way, posing a contrast, or developing the thought further.
- **Reflections on history**: Many psalms look back over things God has done in the writer's national or personal history. You can look back over your own life and history and thank God for all He has done for you and for your nation.

Lesson 1.13

EVALUATION

1. Why is it important to say thank you to God? _____
_____
_____
_____
_____
_____
_____
_____

2. How do you plan to keep track of prayer requests so you can thank God for answered prayer? _____
_____
_____
_____
_____

3. What other blessings besides answered prayer might you praise God for? _____
_____
_____
_____
_____
_____

"God, be merciful to me a sinner" (Luke 18:13).

LESSON 1.14

The Prayer of the Tax Collector

UNIT 1

OVERVIEW

Sometimes all the words can be right, but there's something really dark and dangerous going on in the heart. Jesus' story of the tax collector and the Pharisee illustrates what it means to "pray badly."

SOURCE MATERIAL

- Luke 18:9-14
- Philippians 3:3-11
- Psalm 51
- Proverbs 6:16-19

ACTIVITES

1. A Modern Pharisee. Imagine Jesus' story of the Pharisee and the tax collector (Luke 18:9-14) were to happen in your town today.

What sort of person would be the Pharisee? Who is respected in our culture? Who is considered holy? _____
_____
_____
_____
_____

What sort of person would be the tax collector? Who is despised in our culture? Whom do people look down upon? Whom do they pity? _____
_____
_____
_____
_____

Unit 1: Following Jesus the Priest

What sorts of things might the modern Pharisee pray about? _____
_____
_____
_____
_____
_____
_____
_____
_____

Now….Do you have any of those modern Pharisee traits? Do you sometimes let yourself think that you are not like other people because of these traits? Write in the space below or in your journal, taking some time to thank God for His blessings in your life and confessing where you have taken His blessings for granted and forgotten that they are gifts from God. _____
_____
_____
_____
_____
_____
_____
_____
_____
_____
_____
_____
_____

Lesson 1.14

EVALUATION

1. What's the wrong way to pray? _____

2. What's the right way to pray? _____

3. What does it look like to pray humbly? _____
_____
_____
_____
_____
_____

4. Name a Bible character who started out proud and was humbled by God. _____
_____
_____
_____
_____
_____

"Father, forgive them, for they do not know what they do" (Luke 23:34).

LESSON 1.15

Praying for Enemies and Those Who Have Hurt You

UNIT 1

OVERVIEW

One of the hardest things to do is pray for people we don't like. But we must learn to do it and do it well.

SOURCE MATERIAL

- Matthew 5:43-48
- Romans 12:14

ACTIVITES

1. Identifying Your Enemies. In the space below or in your journal, make a list of...

<u>Corporate Enemies</u>: These are people or groups of people that Christians typically don't like. Also, you can list groups of people that tend to hate Christians. _____

_____
_____
_____
_____
_____
_____
_____
_____
_____
_____
_____
_____

Unit 1: Following Jesus the Priest

Individual Enemies: This is anyone or any group who has hurt, mistreated, or hates you or those you are close to. _____

_____

_____

_____

_____

_____

2. Praying for Your Enemies.

Corporate Enemies: Brainstorm some ideas of how you can pray for the corporate enemies you listed. Then write out a prayer for one of these corporate enemies. _____

_____

_____

_____

_____

_____

_____

_____

_____

_____

_____

_____

_____

_____

_____

Lesson 1.15

Individual Enemies:

First, pray the following prayer: "Abundantly save, O Lord, and have mercy on those I have offended by my sin or carelessness, knowingly or unknowingly, and led away from You. Do not let them perish for my sake, but visit, comfort, strengthen and heal them, and restore them to the joy of Your salvation. Abundantly save, O Lord, and have mercy on those who hate me, who harm me, and who offend me. Let me be an image of You before them, that they might come to love You more fully, and not be driven from You by my sin. Forgive their sins and grant them repentance, that they might walk with You; and grant me grace to forgive them, that we might be at peace."

Second, think through the needs of the individual people that you wrote down and write a prayer (in the space below or in your journal) for God's blessing on each particular person.

UNIT 2: FOLLOWING JESUS THE KING

Kingship is about wisdom. For a king of Israel, obedience to the Law was just assumed—each king was required to write his own personal copy of the Law by hand (Deut 17:18). But kings needed more than just the Law, because they had to handle difficult cases every day that were not explicitly covered by the Law. Making case-by-case decisions calls for wisdom, and the revelation written by Israel's early kings (Proverbs, Ecclesiastes, Song of Songs, much of the book of Psalms) reflects their need to know how to follow God's heart in unclear situations and to pass on their understanding to those who would rule after them.

Jesus is the ultimate King. We usually think of Jesus' kingship in terms of the second coming, when He will physically return to earth and rule the planet—and we should. But Jesus also exhibited royal traits in His earthly ministry, making wise decisions in difficult circumstances, speaking in parables and proverbs, as Solomon did. He calls us to follow Him.

Wisdom begins with the fear of the Lord. We must understand the ethical obligations that God has given us as a guide, and so this unit begins with considering our covenantal obligations as children of Adam, Abraham, and God. We then move on to deal with understanding relationships of all kinds—with the nation, family, city, church, and world—and how these come together in a believer's vocation.

For kingly spiritual disciplines, we return to the Lord's Prayer as a pattern for praying wisely, look at some psalms that also help to guide us into wise prayer, and then move into handling conflict and friendships well, concluding with a lesson on friendships with the opposite sex. If you are going to use the optional Unit M on marriage and sexuality, it makes an ideal finish to the kingship unit. (See the Unit Summary for more information on Unit M.)

UNIT 2

2

FOLLOWING JESUS THE KING

God created the earth and everything in it and gave it all to Adam to cultivate and protect (Gen 1:26-31).

LESSON 2.1

Royal Ethics: Children of Adam

UNIT 2

OVERVIEW

As Adam's heirs, we inherit the responsibility to cultivate and protect the earth. This responsibility includes taking care of the earth's people, the animals and the overall environment. Often there are competing demands, and we need God's wisdom to figure out how to balance everyone's needs in a way that properly images God.

SOURCE MATERIAL

- Genesis 1:26-31, 2:15
- Romans 14
- Psalm 104
- Proverbs 18:13

ACTIVITES

1. Animal Testing. Your classroom discussion will partly focus on the ethics of animal testing for cosmetics, personal care and household products. Go to your bathroom and make a list of ten products that you find there (deodorant, toothpaste, cleaners, etc.), using the chart below. Make a note of what company makes each product.

Product	Company	Y/N

Unit 2: Following Jesus the King

Product	Company	Y/N

Now go online and check to see if these companies and products use animal testing. Fill out the third column of your chart, above.

Take this chart with you into class.

2. Royal Ethics Decision Making. Look at each of the following scenarios and discuss the pros and cons of different solutions. Be prepared to discuss your answers with the class.

Extinction Scenario. Red-spotted owls used to be common throughout your area and in several other states, but over the last hundred years their habitat has been destroyed by people clearing forests, building houses, and developing roads. Now there's only one place they live: in and around your town. The red-spotted owl has a range extending for about a hundred miles around the town, but it only breeds in one ten-acre patch of forest. Recently, conservationists have noticed that barred owls (a different breed) have been showing up in the breeding area in increasing numbers. They are larger and more aggressive than red-spotted owls, and are beginning to displace the red-spotted owls, outcompeting them for food and nesting spots. Conservationists estimate that, if nothing is done, the barred owls will completely displace the red-spotted owls, and in thirty years, the red-spotted owl will be extinct.

Lesson 2.1

What do you do? Do you try to save the species, or do you let nature take its course? _____
_____
_____
_____
_____
_____
_____
_____
_____
_____

Foie Gras Scenario. Over time, gourmets have discovered that duck or goose liver has a particularly desirable taste and consistency if the liver is very fatty. The liver will get fatter if the birds are well-fed, but to produce the perfect fat liver, the birds need to eat quite a bit more than they naturally would. As a result, farmers have learned how to force-feed the birds. In the last two and a half weeks before slaughtering the birds, they will jam a tube down the bird's throat and pump up to 4 pounds of grain (usually corn boiled with fat) into the bird's stomach, repeating the process two to three times a day. The result is that the bird's liver will swell up many times its natural size, giving it a wonderful flavor and texture. The resulting food, foie gras, is tender and flavorful, a common menu item in gourmet restaurants.

Would you ever eat foie gras? _____

Would you ever be willing to work at a farm that produces foie gras? _____

Should it be legal to make foie gras? Should the government be allowed to tell people what foods they can and can't make? Should the government be allowed to decide what farming practices constitute cruelty to animals? _____
_____
_____
_____
_____

Unit 2: Following Jesus the King

Animal Testing Scenario. Multiple sclerosis slowly destroys the human central nervous system. Although a person with MS is likely to live around 35 years after the first diagnosis (about the same as average life expectancy), more aggressive forms of the disease cause incredible suffering, slowly destroying the victim's nerves and causing loss of muscle control, tingling and numbness, loss of bladder and bowel control, depression, memory loss, seizures, twitching, and more. Imagine that a scientist has developed a possible treatment for multiple sclerosis. If successful, it will reverse the course of the disease. The person will have to take the medicine for the rest of his life, but he can live a normal life with no symptoms. But in order to be sure it's safe, it has to go through a series of tests on lab animals like mice, rats, and pigs. In the course of the testing, many of these animals will suffer, and a number of them will die painful deaths, but if the tests are successful, then the new drug will ease the suffering of thousands of people.

Should we do the tests? Why or why not? _____
_____
_____

What if the testing is not to cure a harmful disease; it's just to see if an eyeliner or a deodorant is safe for use on humans? Should we let animals suffer for that? Would you buy a product that's been tested on animals? _____
_____
_____
_____
_____

If it bothers you that your personal care products might have been tested on animals, are you going to do a little research to find out for sure? Or would you rather just not know about it? _____
_____
_____
_____
_____

Lesson 2.1

EVALUATION

1. Explain your own position on one of the previous scenarios and give three arguments in support of your position.

2. Explain a position you disagree with on one of the previous scenarios and explain three of the arguments in support of that position.

God called Abraham from his home to a place God would show him. Abraham believed God and went (Gen 12:1-6).

LESSON 2.2

Royal Ethics: Children of Abraham by Faith

UNIT 2

OVERVIEW

Believers are children of Abraham by faith, and therefore have Abraham's responsibility to be a blessing to those we meet. Simple to say, but often not so easy to do. This lesson brings students face-to-face with the very first fact of Abraham's story: the gateway to Abraham's blessing was radical faith and persistence in following it.

SOURCE MATERIAL

- Genesis 11:29-12:9

ACTIVITES

1. Return to the Extinction Scenario. Remember the extinction scenario from the previous lesson? In the scenario, the red-spotted owl exists in only one place in the world, and breeds only in this particular ten-acre patch of forest. This time though, the threat is not the barred owl; instead, the threat is mining. The town used to have a couple of manufacturing plants, but the companies have moved all their operations to Mexico, because labor there is so much cheaper. The town is going to die without a new source of income, but there's good news: geologists have discovered a rich deposit of gold near the town. A gold mine would provide wealth and jobs for the whole town. The bad news is the gold is located under the forest land where the owl makes its home. The owners of the land want to mine the gold, but that means cutting down the trees and probably causing the red-spotted owl to go extinct.

What should the town do? Why?_____

_____

_____

_____

_____

Unit 2: Following Jesus the King

What would you do if you were the owner of the land?

2. Missionary Scenario. Imagine that you are a missionary called to Indonesia. Indonesia doesn't allow foreign missionaries, so you are in the country as an English professor, teaching English to a classroom full of Muslim students. One of your students has missed a couple days of class, and when you ask your students if anyone has seen him, they tell you he's in the hospital. You and your partner go to visit, expecting to find him in a hospital room like in the US. No such luck—He's in a huge open area full of maybe a hundred hospital beds. Each patient is surrounded by family and friends. It's crowded, hot and noisy; it takes you a while to even find him in the crowd. When you do find him, he's conscious, but very sick; the doctor says he may not last through the night. He's surrounded by his whole extended family and close friends. You feel that you should pray for God to heal him. But how are you going to go about it?

Do you pray silently in your heart?

Do you very quietly ask him if it's okay to pray for him, and then do it as quietly as possible, so the other people around won't really know what's going on?

Lesson 2.2

Do you pray loudly, publicly, in the name of Jesus? _____
_____
_____

Explain what you would do, and why. _____
_____
_____
_____
_____
_____
_____

3. Friendship Scenario. There's an unpopular kid in your class who has no friends at all, as far as you know. You feel like God is calling you to become friends with this person. At first you just ignored the feeling, but it only got stronger. You have talked with a couple of adults you trust. They both say that it seems like a good thing to do, but it might be harder than you think, and it's really up to you to do what you want. But you continue to feel like this is something that God is calling you to do.

What do you do? Why? _____
_____
_____
_____
_____
_____

Suppose you stepped out and tried to befriend the unpopular kid, but it didn't go well. You've tried several times, and every time you say something nice it seems like he (or she) takes the worst possible interpretation of what you've said. It's like he's determined to find something insulting in anything you say to him. He's suspicious and untrusting. No wonder he doesn't have any friends.

What do you do now? _____
_____
_____

Unit 2: Following Jesus the King

4. Journal Time: Blessings Brainstorm. In your journal or the space below, write down some ideas of what you might do to be an instrument of God's blessing to the people around you. Choose at least one of these ideas and put it into practice.

What are some ways you can be an instrument of God's blessing to those around you? _____

Choose at least one of these ideas. How can you actually put this idea into practice? _____

Lesson 2.2

EVALUATION

1. Explain your own position on one of the previous scenarios and give three arguments in support of your position.

2. Explain a position you disagree with on one of the previous scenarios and explain three of the arguments in support of that position.

Before ascending to heaven, Jesus commissioned His disciples to follow in His footsteps and make disciples of the nations (Matt 28:18-20).

LESSON 2.3

Royal Ethics: Children of God in Christ

UNIT 2

OVERVIEW

Believers are children of God in Christ, and therefore have a responsibility to represent Christ, making disciples throughout the world. But it's one thing to talk about how we're *always* responsible to do this, and another thing entirely to balance it with our other responsibilities. In this lesson, students think through the balancing act.

SOURCE MATERIAL

- Luke 10:25-37
- Matthew 28:18-20
- John 5:19-20, 10:1-5

ACTIVITES

1. Extinction Scenario Revisited. Again we have the same scenario with the red-spotted owl as in Lessons 2.1 and 2.2. This time though, you're caught in the middle between two of your friends. Both of them have been friends with you for a long time. Neither one is a believer, but you've had meaningful conversations about the Lord with both of them in the past year, and they're both close to coming to Christ. One of your friends is a biologist at the local university and is leading the charge to make the land a wildlife preserve and save the red-spotted owl. The other is one of the people who owns the land and wants to put in a gold mine. Both are deeply, personally invested in this issue to the point that they're losing friends over it. What do you do?

Unit 2: Following Jesus the King

2. Friendship Scenario Revisited. Again we have the same scenario as in Lesson 2.2: there's an unpopular kid in your class who has no friends, and you feel that God is calling you to befriend him (or her). However, this person seems determined to misinterpret everything you say and do, and keeps taking offense at you when you're trying to be friendly. You start to feel like there's a good reason this person has no friends. BUT, you know this person is an unbeliever. Does this change anything in the way you relate to him/her? _____

_____

_____

_____

3. Street Evangelism Scenario. Yesterday a Christian friend of yours decided to go out and evangelize people outside the local DMV. He was outside on the sidewalk handing out tracts when a security guard came out and told him he wasn't allowed to do that and he would have to leave. He told the security guard that he was exercising his first-amendment rights and he was not leaving. The security guard insisted that it wasn't a religious thing; it's just that nobody was allowed to hand out pamphlets on the property, no matter what was written in them. Again, the guard told him to leave, but your friend wouldn't leave. A crowd began to gather, and the whole big argument ended up on YouTube for the world to see. The security guard eventually called the cops, and the cops escorted your friend off the property, but didn't arrest him or charge him with anything. Today he wants to go back, and he wants you to go with him.

Do you go? Why or why not? _____

_____

Is he right to go? _____

_____

How does his Christian witness look to the security guard? Does this matter? _____

_____

_____

Is there a way to reach the people he's trying to reach and reach the security guard? _____

_____

_____

Lesson 2.3

EVALUATION

1. Explain your own position on one of the previous scenarios and give three arguments in support of your position.

2. Explain a position you disagree with on one of the previous scenarios and explain three of the arguments in support of that position.

Jesus modeled wise judgement when His disciples were accused of breaking the Sabbath by plucking grain. Jesus knew better and rebuked the religious leaders accordingly (Matt 12:1-8).

LESSON 2.4

Royal Ethics: Formal Debate

UNIT 2

OVERVIEW

Formal debate allows students the opportunity to solidify some of the listening and arguing skills they have been practicing informally in the preceding three lessons.

ACTIVITES

1. Formal Debate Preparation. The key to formal debate is preparing ahead of time. These are the elements of the debate that your team will have to be ready for.

<u>Constructive Speech.</u> Make the case for your position. This is the only time you can introduce new arguments, so get everything you want to say on the table during this time.

- What are the key terms and definitions for your argument?
- What exactly is your position?
- Why should someone agree with you?
- Is there a key example, analogy, or story that will help make your point?

<u>Cross-Examination (if applicable).</u> Ask questions to clarify your opponent's position or reveal contradictions in his argument. You MAY NOT argue with your opponent or make arguments during this time.

- How do you expect your opponent to define his position?
- What questions could you ask that might expose a weakness in his position?

    Don't forget that even though you can prepare for some things your opponent will probably say, you have to respond to what he actually says. Be ready to think on your feet.

<u>Rebuttal.</u> Point out any weaknesses in your opponent's argument. You may not introduce new arguments of your own; this time is only for explaining why your opponent's arguments do not support his position.

- Prepare for rebuttals by anticipating the arguments your opponents might make. Do some research—for most issues, there is a set of standard arguments on both sides. What are the standard arguments for your opponent's position?
- What are some good responses for your opponent's standard arguments?

    Remember that you have to respond to what your opponent actually said, so be prepared to modify your responses.

<u>Closing.</u> Summarize your argument and explain why you won the debate. You MAY NOT introduce any new arguments at this point; you can only work with what's already been presented.

- Prepare a quick summary of your argument as it was presented in the constructive speech. You're going to modify it some, but it's good to have a general speech ready and then modify from there.
- Be ready to drop any arguments that you feel like your opponent shot down and to emphasize any arguments your opponent didn't answer effectively.
- Make a quick summary of your rebuttals and recap why your opponent didn't make his case.

DEBATE PREPARATION

As a group, fill in the pages below, so you are prepared for your debate.

Who Will Do Each Segment?

Remember to think about the strengths of each of your teammates. The constructives are planned ahead of time; the people who deliver those don't have to think on their feet. The people who do the rebuttals will have some prepared responses, but will have to modify them on the fly and fill in with counterarguments for whatever arguments you didn't anticipate ahead of time. The closing can be partly planned ahead of time, but it also has some improvised parts. It's also the last thing your audience will hear from you, so you might want to choose your strongest, most confident speaker for the close.

First Constructive:_____

Second Constructive:_____

First Rebuttal:_____

Second Rebuttal:_____

Closing:_____

Lesson 2.4

Building Your Constructive Speeches

What are your arguments for your position?

What order would be best to present them?

Which arguments should go in your first constructive? Which in your second? _____

_____
_____
_____
_____
_____
_____
_____
_____
_____
_____
_____

Building Your Rebuttals

Of course you have to build most of your rebuttals on the fly, because you have to be responding to what your opponent actually said. But it will be a lot easier if you can prepare a little.

What arguments do you expect your opponent to use? _____

_____
_____
_____
_____
_____
_____
_____
_____
_____
_____
_____

How would you respond to them? _____
_____
_____
_____
_____
_____
_____
_____
_____
_____
_____
_____
_____

Building Your Closing

The job of the closing is to show why you won the debate. You can plan some of this in advance, and the rest you'll have to improvise.

What were your main arguments for your own position? _____
_____
_____
_____
_____
_____
_____
_____
_____
_____
_____

Unit 2: Following Jesus the King

How did your opponent fail to counter them (how were your opponent's rebuttals ineffective)?

How did your opponent's arguments for his position fail. (Recap your rebuttal speeches).

What is the *very last* thing you want to leave in the minds of your audience?

Lesson 2.4

DEBRIEF DAY

After the debate, answer the following questions to reflect on your debate experience. Be prepared to discuss your answers in class.

1. What did you think about the issue before you started working on it? _____
_____
_____

2. How did your preparation for the debate change your thinking? _____
_____
_____
_____

3. Did hearing the other team's arguments change your thinking at all? How? _____
_____
_____
_____

4. How do you think about the issue now that you've had a little time to consider it? _____
_____
_____
_____

5. Why do other people disagree with your position on this issue? Do you understand their reasoning?
_____
_____
_____

6. Would your opponents agree with your answer to the previous question? If not, why not? _____
_____
_____
_____

"Render therefore to Caesar the things that are Caesar's, and to God the things that are God's" (Matt 22:21).

LESSON 2.5

Christian Worldview: Relating to Your Nation

UNIT 2

OVERVIEW

Christians have always had an...interesting...relationship with national governments. At our best, we are their best subjects, because we obey the laws and love our neighbors. At the same time, we're their most troublesome subjects, because we recognize a higher authority. Getting ourselves clear on a Christian relationship to national government will also lay the biblical groundwork for understanding our relationships with other human authorities.

SOURCE MATERIAL

- Matthew 22:15-22, 28:18
- Acts 4:1-31 and Psalm 2
- 1 Peter 2:11-17
- Romans 13
- 1 Timothy 2:1-4
- Proverbs 16:10-15

ACTIVITES

1. Civil Disobedience Comparison. After reading Henry David Thoreau's essay, "Civil Disobedience," use the table below to compare Thoreau's view of civil government with the biblical view.

Thoreau's View of Civil Government	Biblical View of Civil Government

Unit 2: Following Jesus the King

2. Praying for Your Leaders. Paul requires us to pray for "kings and all in authority" (1 Tim 2:2). For us in America, this means praying for the President. Do some research so you can pray intelligently. (If you live in another country than America, you may choose to pray for whomever is the leader of that country).

Who is the President? _____

List the members of his immediate family and their ages. _____

_____

Are the President's parents still alive? If so, what are their names? _____

_____

What are some current challenges facing the President? _____

_____

_____

_____

_____

What would it look like for God's will to be done "on earth as it is in heaven" in these challenges? _____

_____

_____

_____

_____

_____

_____

_____

_____

Take some time to pray for God's will to be done in the President's life. Don't forget to pray for a strong marriage, strong relationships with his children, and for him to honor his parents.

Lesson 2.5

EVALUATION

1. Who has all authority? _____

2. If Jesus has all authority, then why would we obey the government? _____

3. What is the big principle that Jesus taught about civil government? _____

4. What are some of the reasons Paul gives to obey the civil government? _____
_____
_____
_____
_____

5. Is it right to resist the civil government anytime they are doing something wrong? _____
_____

6. When is it right to disobey the civil government? _____
_____
_____
_____

7. What else should we do for civil government? _____
   Why should we pray for them? _____
_____
_____
_____

"And Jesus increased in wisdom and stature, and in favor with God and men" (Luke 2:52).

LESSON 2.6

Christian Worldview: Relating to Your Family

UNIT 2

OVERVIEW

A thoroughly Christian worldview works in terms of relationships more than in terms of issues. Christians have a variety of relationships that we need to contemplate, but the very first set of relationships God gives us is the family. In this lesson, we focus not on the family in the abstract, but on God's specific role for the student as a Christian child in a particular family.

SOURCE MATERIAL

- Luke 2:52
- 1 Samuel 2:26, 3
- Matthew 21:28-32
- Proverbs 1:8-9, 4:1-9, 10:1, 15:20, 20:20, 28:24, 29:3, 30:17
- *He Shall Crush His Head, Part 2,* Lesson 1.4

ACTIVITES

1. How to Grow Up. You've spent this lesson giving attention to how Jesus grew up and what it means to mature as part of a family. List some areas where you need to mature as part of your family.

Unit 2: Following Jesus the King

Choose one of the things you listed above. Write a prayer bringing it before God, confessing your sin, and asking Him what He wants you to do about it today. _____

_____

_____

_____

_____

_____

_____

So...how'd it go? What did God ask you to do, and did you do it? How did it work out? _____

_____

_____

_____

_____

_____

_____

2. Tale of Two Sons. Read the parable of the two sons and the vineyard in Matthew 21:28-32. Using this parable as a starting point, write your own version of this story. Expand the story, add details to it, and then continue telling the story all the way to the end. What happens to each son? As an added challenge, work in as many proverbs as you can into your story. _____

_____

_____

_____

_____

_____

Lesson 2.6

Unit 2: Following Jesus the King

3. Change One Thing. After all this talk on what it means to grow up well, you have surely encountered a few things that you need to change in your own life.

Pick one of these things and write down how you are going to make a change. _____

_____
_____
_____
_____
_____
_____
_____
_____
_____
_____

After making the change, write a paragraph about your experience below. _____

_____
_____
_____
_____
_____
_____
_____
_____
_____
_____
_____
_____

Lesson 2.6

EVALUATION

1. What does it mean that Jesus (and Samuel) increased in wisdom? _____
_____
_____
_____

2. What is involved in increasing in stature? Doesn't that happen automatically? _____
_____
_____
_____

3. What did Jesus and Samuel do to increase in favor with God? _____
_____
_____

4. What is involved in increasing in favor with man? _____
_____
_____

5. Name two characteristics of a good child according to Proverbs. _____
_____
_____

"And many of the Samaritans of that city believed in Him because of the word of the woman who testified" (John 4:39).

LESSON 2.7

Christian Worldview: Relating to Your City

UNIT 2

OVERVIEW

Relating to the community in which we live is a critical skill for Christians. We can choose a life of isolation, in which we refrain from human contact with the people we meet every day, or we can engage them in order to show love to them.

SOURCE MATERIAL

- Matthew 22:35-40

ACTIVITES

1. Stock Interactions Brainstorming. We have certain things we say all the time without thinking. One of the most common is this:

"Hey, how are you?"

"Fine. You?"

"Fine."

What other interactions do you have in a typical day that are completely automatic? (If it helps, think of things that your parents have taught you to say automatically in social situations.)

Unit 2: Following Jesus the King

2. Breaking Stock Interactions Brainstorm. The interactions you listed above are not pointless; they're polite. For example, many people would consider "How are you?" a polite way of acknowledging someone's presence. But these automatic interactions also provide an opportunity to have an affect on people by breaking their expectations. For example, instead of asking, "How are you?" you might ask, "What's awesome about your day so far?" in order to prompt a person to be grateful for the good things in his or her day.

As a group, come up with three ways to break each one of the automatic interactions you listed above. Remember, the point is not just to have fun, but to make the other person feel loved and cared for. _____

_____

_____

_____

_____

_____

_____

_____

_____

3. Breaking Stock Interactions Practice. After your teacher leads you in the role-play activity with the ideas you came up with, write your thoughts about the activity below. How did it work? _____

_____

_____

_____

_____

_____

_____

_____

_____

Lesson 2.7

EVALUATION

1. Give some examples of social patterns (or stock patterns) of relating to people that help us avoid acknowledging each other. _____
_____
_____

2. Describe two occasions in the last [day/two days/week] where you've deliberately broken a social pattern in order to make someone feel cared for. _____
_____
_____
_____
_____
_____
_____

3. What is the second greatest commandment? _____
_____

4. What are machinery people? _____
_____

5. What are scenery people? _____
_____

The Church is the Spirit-filled body of Christ (Acts 2:2-4).

LESSON 2.8

Christian Worldview: Relating to the Church

UNIT 2

OVERVIEW

Many Christians have a really hard time with church, either because of a bad experience or just because they just don't feel connected to God in church. They feel more connected to God playing music or spending time outdoors than they do in church. Christians need to recapture a vibrant vision of the Church as the body of Christ—His hands in the world, His body building itself up through Him, and His people gathered before the throne in praise.

SOURCE MATERIAL

- Revelation 21-22
- Matthew 28:18-20
- John 13-17
- Hebrews, various texts (see activities)

ACTIVITES

1. Local Church Shortcomings. Get out your Bible and read the last few chapters. What will the Church be like in the end? In the space below, list the traits you observe.

Unit 2: Following Jesus the King

Which of these traits does your local church have now? Which ones is your local church lacking?

Pick one of the traits your local church is lacking that is particularly important to you. Write a prayer below asking God to bring out that trait in your church. Then ask Him how you can help.

Lesson 2.8

2. Where Are We? Read the following verses from Hebrews and answer the questions associated with each.

- Hebrews 1:13

Who does God say this to? _____

Where is God's right hand? Where is Jesus sitting? _____
_____

- Hebrews 2:17

What does the high priest do? _____
_____
_____

- Hebrews 4:14-16

When we come before the throne of grace, where are we going? _____
_____
_____

- Hebrews 6:17-20

Where does our hope go? _____
_____

What in the world does that mean? What veil? _____
_____
_____

What is a forerunner? _____
_____

What does that mean for us? _____
_____
_____

Quick review: where is He? Where are we? _____
_____

Unit 2: Following Jesus the King

- Hebrews 8:1-6

Where does Jesus minister? _____
_____

What is the relationship between the heavenly tabernacle and the earthly one? _____
_____
_____
_____

- Hebrews 10:19-25

Is the author challenging them to do something individually, in their hearts, or is he challenging them to do something outward, something visible? _____
_____
_____

- Hebrews 12:18-24

Where have we not come? _____
_____

Where have we come? _____
_____

- Hebrews 13:12-16

What are the sacrifices that we offer to God? _____
_____
_____

Do we just do this when we come together? _____
_____
_____

EVALUATION

1. What is the standard by which we evaluate the Church? _____

2. What does it mean when my local church falls short of the standard? _____

3. What is the difference between doing church/going to church and being the Church? _____

4. What are the three key relationships in the Church? _____

5. As the Church, what's our duty in our relationship with the world? _____

6. How do we learn how to do that duty? _____

7. As the Church, what's our duty in our relationship with each other? _____

8. As the Church, what's our duty in our relationship with God? _____

Wherever Paul went, he caused strong reactions, some good, some bad. In Ephesus, many came to the Lord and burned their books of sorcery... at the same time, many feared Paul's message would disrupt their idol making business and started a riot (Acts 19).

LESSON 2.9

Christian Worldview: Relating to Your World

UNIT 2

OVERVIEW

God loves the whole world, and a Christian has no right to be an isolationist. In order to be the image of God in the world, we have to be engaged with the world, willing to hold its people up in prayer and seek the good of others regardless of where they live.

SOURCE MATERIAL

- 1 Timothy 2:1-4
- Matthew 9:35-38
- Psalm 2
- Galatians 6:10
- A current news item from Voice of the Martyrs

ACTIVITES

1. Praying for Persecuted Believers. Go to the Voice of the Martyrs website (www.persecution.com). Read through a few current news articles and select one that resonates for you. List some things you could pray for about this situation. What do you know is God's will in this situation? What do you want to happen?

Unit 2: Following Jesus the King

Write a prayer that incorporates the things you listed above and pray it to the Lord. _____
_____
_____
_____
_____
_____
_____

2. Praying for America's Enemies. In the space below, list some enemies of our country. _____
_____
_____

Write a prayer below for the gospel to reach these enemies so that they not only come to faith in Christ, but are transformed into disciples of Christ. _____
_____
_____
_____
_____
_____

Write a prayer below for our own country, that our nation would also come to faith in Christ and be transformed into sold-out disciples of Christ. _____
_____
_____
_____
_____
_____
_____

EVALUATION

1. As a result of this study, how will the reality that "Jesus is King" affect your Americanism and everyday life? _____

2. How has taking the time to diligently pray for the nations of the world, persecuted believers, and America's enemies affected you in the last week? What conversations or lessons spawned from this project? Is it something you will continue to do? Why or why not? _____

3. What is a Christian's obligation to the world? How will you fulfill that obligation? _____

Part of Solomon's calling was to build the temple. God provided him with the people, talent and resources to make that huge project happen (1 Kgs 6).

LESSON 2.10

Christian Worldview: Your Vocation

UNIT 2

OVERVIEW

God has created a world with endless possibilities for the Christian: a vast potential network of relationships, organizational ties and personal commitments. These opportunities, however, are constrained by where and to whom a person is born, what spiritual gifts, personal abilities and resources he has. Within these constraints, God has a vocation (or calling) that He has planned for every individual. But here's the catch: God doesn't generally give us a roadmap showing His plan for our lives. Rather, He calls us to a process of discovering our place in community, work, and various commitments *on the way*. And as we discover what God's calling is for us in the world, we get to know God Himself!

SOURCE MATERIAL

- Genesis 1:26-31, 2:15
- Matthew 25:14-30

ACTIVITES

1. Vocation Interview. Choose a Christian adult to interview. Make sure it's someone over 40, at least—over 60 would be better, and over 80 would be great, if you can manage it. Here are a few questions to get you started.

What jobs have you held?_____
_____
_____

How did God prepare you for each of those jobs?_____
_____
_____

What did you learn from each job?_____
_____

Unit 2: Following Jesus the King

What significant things did you do outside your job? _____
_____
_____

Looking back, what would you say has been God's calling for you? _____
_____
_____

Ask lots of follow-up questions. Hear your interviewee's story. Come to class prepared to share what you learned. _____
_____
_____
_____
_____
_____
_____

2. Gratitude List. In the space below, write a list of everything you can think of that God has given you that is relevant to your calling. This includes relationships, riches, opportunities (education, for example), gifts and abilities. _____
_____
_____
_____
_____
_____
_____

Now spend some time praying through that list and thanking God for what He has given you. Being a good steward of God's gifts starts with gratitude.

Lesson 2.10

EVALUATION

1. What does the word "vocation" mean? _____

2. What kinds of jobs does God call people to? _____
_____

3. How does God tend to reveal His plan for our lives? _____
_____
_____

4. What does it mean to be a good steward? _____
_____

5. What kinds of things are we called to be good stewards of? _____
_____

6. Does God always call us to do things that He has equipped us for and given us the resources to accomplish? _____
_____
_____

Jesus is our example and teacher regarding how to pray.

LESSON 2.11

Royal Disciplines: Praying in the Manner of the Lord's Prayer

UNIT 2

OVERVIEW

Praying the Lord's Prayer word for word is a priestly discipline (Lesson 1.10); learning to pray *in the manner of* the Lord's prayer is a kingly discipline. There are numerous ways to use the Lord's Prayer as a model for prayer. In this lesson we will explore two models for applying the Lord's Prayer to specific prayer requests.

SOURCE MATERIAL

- Matthew 6:9-13
- Luke 11:1-4

ACTIVITES

1. Modeling the Lord's Prayer. Your teacher will model for your class how to pray in the manner of the Lord's Prayer. Follow your teacher's instructions to fill in two different ways of using the Prayer.

Praying the Lord's Prayer as a set of categories

Our Father, who art in heaven._____

_____

_____

_____

Hallowed be Thy name._____

_____

_____

_____

Thy kingdom come._____

_____

Unit 2: Following Jesus the King

_____

_____

Thy will be done on earth as it is in heaven._____

_____

_____

_____

Give us this day our daily bread._____

_____

_____

_____

Forgive us our trespasses, as we forgive those who trespass against us._____

_____

_____

_____

And lead us not into temptation, but deliver us from evil._____

_____

_____

_____

For Thine is the kingdom, and the power, and the glory forever and ever._____

_____

_____

_____

Praying one specific situation using the Lord's Prayer as a lens

Our Father, who art in heaven._____

_____

_____

_____

Hallowed be Thy name.

Thy kingdom come.

Thy will be done on earth as it is in heaven.

Give us this day our daily bread.

Forgive us our trespasses, as we forgive those who trespass against us.

And lead us not into temptation, but deliver us from evil.

For Thine is the kingdom, and the power, and the glory forever and ever.

Unit 2: Following Jesus the King

2. Pray It. You may already be praying the Lord's Prayer word for word on a regular basis. If you are, that's great, and this activity will build on what you're already doing. Continue to pray the Lord's Prayer word for word; then use the Lord's Prayer either as a set of categories to pray through whatever the Lord lays on your heart, or as a set of lenses for praying through a particular situation. Make a commitment for how often you will pray (either daily or weekly) and write your commitment below. _____

_____

_____

3. Journal Time: The Lord's Prayer. Now that you have had a few days to pray in the manner of the Lord's Prayer, read back over your Journal Time activity from Lesson 1.10. What new insights do you have? In what ways do you now have a deeper understanding of the Prayer, a changed view of God, or a fresh way of looking at the world around you?_____

Lesson 2.11

EVALUATION

1. Did Jesus give the Lord's Prayer as a model or as a rote prayer to be prayed word for word? _____
_____

2. What is the advantage of having a set of categories to pray through?_____
_____

3. What is the significance of beginning the prayer with, "Our Father, who art in heaven"? _____
_____
_____

4. What does "hallowed be Thy name" mean? _____
_____
_____

5. Give some examples of what kind of specific things you might pray in the "Thy kingdom come..." section of the Lord's prayer._____
_____

6. How do you decide what you can pray for in the "Thy kingdom come" section?_____
_____

7. Besides literal food, what might you pray for in the "Give us this day our daily bread" section? _____
_____

8. Does it scare you to pray "forgive us our trespasses *as we forgive those who trespass against us*"? Would you be happy to have God treat your sins the way you treat other people's sins?_____
_____

9. Give some examples of what kind of specific things you might pray in the "Lead us not into temptation..." section of the Lord's prayer._____
_____

10. Why do we close the Prayer with "For Thine is the kingdom, and the power, and the glory, forever"? _____
_____

One of the results of being filled with the Holy Spirit is singing and praying the Psalms (Eph 5:18-19).

LESSON 2.12

Royal Disciplines: Praying the Psalms

UNIT 2

OVERVIEW

The Psalms are the prayers of a king. Praying psalms helps us address God as kings addressing their master and transforms us by giving us the words and thoughts of godly people of the past.

SOURCE MATERIAL

- The book of Psalms
- Ephesians 5:18-19
- Colossians 3:16
- James 5:13

Through the Psalms in a Month (Book of Common Prayer)		
Day	Morning	Evening
1	1-5	6-8
2	9-11	12-14
3	15-17	18
4	19-21	22-23
5	24-26	27-29
6	30-31	32-34
7	35-36	37
8	38-40	41-43
9	44-46	47-49
10	50-52	53-55
11	56-58	59-61
12	62-64	65-67
13	68	69-70
14	71-72	73-74

Day	Morning	Evening
15	75-77	78
16	79-81	82-85
17	86-88	89
18	90-92	93-94
19	95-97	98-101
20	102-103	104
21	105	106
22	107	108-109
23	110-113	114-115
24	116-118	119:1-32
25	119:33-72	119:73-104
26	119:105-144	119:145-176
27	120-125	126-131
28	132-135	136-138
29	139-140	141-143
30	144-146	147-150

Unit 2: Following Jesus the King

ACTIVITES

1. Verse One. Lots of people need some help getting started praying the Psalms. Here is a useful activity to get you started. Read through the first verse of each psalm (1:1, 2:1, 3:1, and so on). Look for a verse that seems to reflect how you're feeling, that fascinates you, that resonates somehow for you. When you find that verse, spend some time praying through that particular psalm.

Which psalm did you choose?_____

What made you choose that psalm?_____

_____

_____

_____

_____

Write down some thoughts below about praying through the psalm. Did you feel the same way afterwards as when you started? Did the psalm say anything that surprised you? Did it say anything that made you uncomfortable?_____

_____

_____

_____

_____

1. Pray It. Pick a psalm that you like (it can be the same psalm as in Activity 1), and make a commitment to pray this psalm on a regular basis. This could be praying it every day or every week.

What psalm have you chosen to pray on a regular basis?_____

Why did you choose this psalm?_____

_____

_____

_____

How has praying this psalm affected you? _____
_____
_____
_____
_____
_____

If you are ambitious, you can use the chart on page 141 to guide you in praying through the entire book of Psalms in one month.

EVALUATION

1. Why were the Psalms originally written? _____
_____
_____

2. How has the Church used the book of Psalms throughout Church history? _____
_____
_____
_____

3. What does Ephesians 5:18 say that Christians are to be filled with? What does this have to do with praying psalms? _____
_____
_____
_____
_____

"Truly I tell you, among those born of women there has not risen anyone greater than John the Baptist; yet whoever is least in the kingdom of heaven is greater than he" (Matt 11:11).

LESSON 2.13

Royal Disciplines: Basics of Being Great in the Kingdom of God

UNIT 2

OVERVIEW

According to Revelation 5:9-10, Christ will make us kings and priests to our God. We've talked about being priests earlier in the year. In order to prepare for the day when Christ makes us kings and queens, we must learn to be great in His kingdom. In this lesson, we'll see how Jesus taught His disciples the basics of becoming great in the kingdom of God.

SOURCE MATERIAL

- Matthew 18:1-14

ACTIVITES

1. Outline and Summarize Matthew 18:1-14. Read Matthew 18:1-14. Then write an outline of Jesus' speech below.

Unit 2: Following Jesus the King

Write a one-paragraph summary of Jesus' answer to the question: "Who is greatest in the kingdom of heaven?" What might be the common thread that holds Jesus' answer all together? _____

_____
_____
_____
_____
_____
_____

2. Our Treatment of Sin. Brainstorm some sins our culture tolerates. Write a list in the space below and be prepared to discuss your list in class. _____

_____
_____
_____
_____
_____
_____
_____

After discussing our treatment of sin as a class, write in your journal or the space below, reflecting on your own treatment of sin. _____

_____
_____
_____
_____
_____
_____
_____

EVALUATION

1. What was the question that started Jesus' discussion with the disciples about who is the greatest?
_____
_____

2. And who *is* greatest in the kingdom of heaven? _____
_____
_____
_____

3. What is the point of being like the little child? _____
_____

4. What is the point of cutting off a hand or foot to prevent sin? _____
_____

5. What is the point of the parable of the lost sheep? _____
_____
_____

6. What would it look like to leave the 99 and go pursue the 1 in your life? _____
_____
_____

Jacob went to great lengths to heal his broken relationship with Esau, and it worked (Gen 32-33).

LESSON 2.14

Royal Disciplines: Handling Conflict Well

UNIT 2

OVERVIEW

Jesus continued to answer the disciples' question about greatness in the kingdom. The rest of His answer to this question has to do with how we handle conflict. Do we preserve others' character and reputation, or do we gossip about and sabotage one another?

SOURCE MATERIAL

- Matthew 18:15-17, 21-35
- Matthew 5:23-24
- Psalms 55, 142

ACTIVITES

1. Journal Time: Confession. Jesus said that when someone offends you, you should tell no one until you've taken the time to speak to the person about it yourself.

Take some time to think over the last week: how often have you shared your problems with someone or your bad opinion of someone with others without talking with the person first? If you can think of times you've done this recently, list them in your journal or the space below._____

_____
_____
_____
_____
_____
_____

Telling others before you address the person who offended you is direct disobedience to Jesus' command. It's sin. If you listed some situations above where you've done this, take some time to confess your sin to the Lord.

Unit 2: Following Jesus the King

When you spread a bad report about someone without talking to that person first, it's not just a sin against God. It's also a sin against that person. If you've done this, go and confess your sin to that person. In the space below or in your journal, make a list of the people you need to talk to below, and check them off when you're done.

2. Journal Time: Grudge Check. Take some time to consider whether you are harboring a grudge against someone over some past event. Then read Psalms 55 and 142. How can you pray about this situation like the psalmist does? Write in your journal or the space below—talk to God about how this person has wronged you, instead of gossiping with one of your close friends.

Lesson 2.14

EVALUATION

1. What is the context of Jesus' discussion about handling conflict? _____
_____
_____

2. If I think my friend has sinned against me, what should I do? _____
_____

3. What if he won't listen? _____
_____

4. What if he still won't listen? _____
_____

5. What if my church leadership won't do anything? _____
_____
_____

Joseph was loyal to his brothers even after they had betrayed him (Gen 45).

LESSON 2.15

Being a Good Friend

UNIT 2

OVERVIEW

Being a good friend is about understanding our loyalties and then incarnating those loyalties in the way that we live. Sorting out our loyalties and how to live them is not a simple matter, because we owe everybody *something*; it takes divine wisdom. It is also not a simple matter because sin clouds our judgment, especially when it comes to dealing with people who have much more—or much less—than we do. So being a good friend also requires being willing to face the sin in our own hearts and repent of it.

SOURCE MATERIAL

- Deuteronomy 5:16
- Matthew 22:35-40
- Galatians 6:7-10

ACTIVITES

1. Concentric Rings. In the circles below, map your relationships, with immediate family the closest and strangers furthest out.

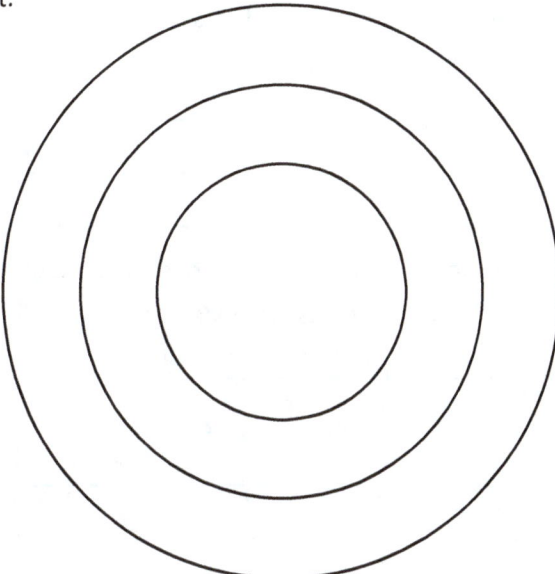

Unit 2: Following Jesus the King

Once you have your relationships mapped out, answer the following questions, and be prepared to discuss your answers in class.

For whom do you drop everything because the person needs help? _____
_____
_____

Whom would you invite to spend the night in your house? (What if the person was going to have to sleep outside under a bridge if you didn't invite him/her in? Does that make a difference?) _____
_____
_____

To whom would you feed a meal? For whom would you be willing to give up your own meal in order that the other person could eat? _____
_____

2. Journal Time: Greater and Lesser Blessing. In your journal or the space below, list some ways that God blesses people (physical attractiveness, intelligence, money, etc.). Put a star by the three types of blessing that are most important to you. _____
_____
_____

For those three blessings you starred, choose the one that is most important to you. Then list one person you know who is more blessed than you are in that area and one person who is less blessed than you are. _____
_____
_____

Are you happy for the person who has more, or are you jealous? Take a moment to thank God for His blessing on that person (and if necessary, to confess your jealousy). _____
_____
_____
_____
_____

Lesson 2.15

Think of one way you might share your greater blessing with the person who has less than you. Write your thoughts below. _____
_____
_____
_____
_____
_____
_____

Do you think you'll actually do it? Why or why not?_____
_____
_____
_____
_____

EVALUATION

1. What is loyalty?_____

2. Who do you consider "your people"? Start with those whom you consider your closest people and work out from there._____
_____

3. Who defines your loyalties?_____
_____

4. Why must we honor our people?_____

5. Is our calling to honor our parents dependent on their behavior? _____
_____

6. What is courtesy? _____

7. To whom do you owe courtesy?_____
_____

8. How should you treat your friends who have been blessed in greater ways than you have? _____
_____

Jesus made friends with a Samaritan woman that He met at a well (John 4).

LESSON 2.16

Opposite Sex Friendships

UNIT 2

OVERVIEW

God made the world in such a way that it takes men and women working together as a team to understand it well and know what to do. Opposite gender friendships can be dangerous and frustrating, but learning to handle them well is an essential life skill. The biblical instructions for how to act in a marriage provide us with some clues for how to understand the opposite gender's needs, so we can love one another wisely.

SOURCE MATERIAL

- Ephesians 5:22-33
- Proverbs 22:3
- Ecclesiastes 3:1-8

ACTIVITES

1. Opposite Gender, Opposite Thoughts. Answer the following questions, and be prepared to discuss your answers.

If you are having difficulty with a homework problem what do you tend to do about it? _____
_____
_____

What would you do if you saw someone (of your own sex) trying to do something (a project, craft, or skill) that you were good at, how would you go about helping them? Or would you even try to help them? _____
_____

If you have several friends over for a sleepover, what do you stay up late doing? _____
_____
_____
_____

Unit 2: Following Jesus the King

If someone you aren't friends with insults you, how do you respond? _____
_____
_____

If someone you are friends with insults you, how do you respond? _____
_____
_____

In sports, how would you describe the relationship you have with your teammates? The opposing team? _____
_____

Describe what you hope that your life might look like in twenty years. _____
_____
_____

What's something you're really good at? _____
_____
_____

2. Journal Time: Opposite Gender Friendships. Two major temptations we face in opposite gender friendships are 1) having friends of only one gender and 2) lust. Spend some time writing in your journals or the space below about your own experience with these temptations. If you find that you only have friends of one gender, write in your journal, asking God to provide healthy friendships of the opposite gender. If your temptation is lust, write a confession to God. _____
_____
_____
_____
_____
_____
_____

Lesson 2.16

EVALUATION

1. What should our basic orientation as Christians be toward opposite sex relationships? _____
_____
_____
_____

2. What principle of love builds a foundation for godly relationships with the opposite sex *and* prepares us to treat our spouse right when we do get married?_____
_____

3. Why do we need friends of both sexes?_____
_____
_____

4. What are the two key temptations to avoid in opposite sex friendships?_____
_____

5. What kinds of things might damage an opposite sex friendship? _____
_____
_____

6. What particular difficulties are associated with opposite sex friendships?_____
_____
_____

Marriage involves three persons: God, a man, and a woman. "Then the rib which the Lord God had taken from man He made into a woman, and He brought her to the man" (Gen 2:22).

LESSON M-1

Sex in Marriage

UNIT 2

OVERVIEW

We can't have a biblical discussion about sex by itself; in the Bible, the context of sex is marriage. So we begin in the garden of Eden with God's design for marriage: one man and one woman, for life. From there, we move forward through the Ten Commandments and into the New Testament teaching of Jesus and Paul, where we learn that God's real purpose in marriage is to make an earthly image of Christ and the Church. Sex has its place within that image as an intense physical picture of love, communion and commitment. Sex is glorious and powerful, and, like anything powerful, it's highly dangerous. Marriage is the only container that can safely hold it.

SOURCE MATERIAL

- Genesis 2
- Exodus 20
- Exodus 22:16-17
- Leviticus 20:10
- Ephesians 5:22-33

ACTIVITES

1. Interview. Your assignment is to interview a Christian couple whom you already know who has a good marriage. Take notes on the answers you get, and be prepared to discuss your interview with the class. Below is a list of questions to ask.

What is the story of how you met?

Unit 2: Following Jesus the King

What did your courtship or dating experience look like? Share any particular stories that stick out in your memory as being important to your developing relationship. _____
_____
_____
_____

How long was it from when you met to when you got married? _____
_____
_____
_____

When did you know you were "in love" and ready to get married? Did both of you get there at the same time? How did it all come together that you finally got married? _____
_____
_____
_____

What was the biggest blessing for each of you after you got married? The biggest adjustment? _____
_____
_____
_____

To the extent to which you are willing to share, what is the most difficult challenge you have had to overcome as a married couple? How did you overcome it? _____
_____
_____
_____
_____

How does your love for each other now compare to the beginning of your marriage? _____
_____
_____

Lesson M-1

Describe the difference between being single and being married. _____
_____
_____

What are you most looking forward to in the future of your marriage? What do you think life will be like as a married couple at your 50th anniversary? _____
_____
_____

EVALUATION

1. What did God say after He created Adam, but before He created Eve? _____
_____

2. How many persons are involved in a marriage? _____
_____

3. Who gives meaning to marriage? _____
_____

4. Summarize God's design for marriage. _____
_____

5. What were the consequences for pre-marital sex in the Old Testament? _____
_____
_____
_____

6. What were the consequences for adultery in the Old Testament? _____

7. Why were the consequences so serious? _____
_____
_____

8. Ultimately, what is marriage supposed to be a picture of? _____
_____
_____

God loves to make beauty out of brokenness. Lot's sinful relationships with his daughters caused many problems; but ultimately, God used Lot's sin for good by bringing Ruth, a descendant of Lot, to marry Boaz—a marriage that would be in Jesus' line.

LESSON M-2

Why Wait?

UNIT 2

OVERVIEW

The Bible teaches us that God can redeem the worst sexual mistakes. The Bible also teaches us that harsh consequences can come from sexual disobedience, but great rewards come from a devoted marital relationship. Sex is not a sin to avoid, but a blessing to wait for. We also want your students to understand that God can redeem any poor decisions your students may have already made in this area.

SOURCE MATERIAL

- Proverbs 5, 7
- Song of Songs
- Genesis 19:30-38, Ruth, Matthew 1:1-6, 1 Kings 14:21, 31

ACTIVITES

1. Departures from Design. In this lesson we have focused on what Proverbs has to say about the perils of abusing God's good gifts through adultery and fornication. There are also numerous Bible stories that address the consequences of this kind of sin. We used one example, Lot; but there are many others. Think of as many departures from God's design as you can and write them in the right hand column on the following page. Then, in the left hand column, write what the consequences were for each of these sins.

Unit 2: Following Jesus the King

Examples of Sexual Sin in the Bible	Consequences for These Sexual Sins

2. Split Assignment.

- **Boys:** Make a flip-book animation of Proverbs 7 (stick figures are fine). Be literal. Proverbs is explicit and gruesome. Make sure to do it justice, and don't be shy about using the red ink.
- **Girls:** Compare and contrast the Song of Songs with a romantic book, movie, or song you're familiar with. How are they alike? How are they different?

_____
_____
_____
_____
_____
_____
_____

EVALUATION

1. Name three biblical examples of marriages that departed from God's design. What were the consequences? _____

2. When it comes to sex and love, what is the basic biblical command to young men who are not yet married? _____

3. When it comes to sex and love, what is the basic biblical command to girls who are not yet married? _____

4. How did God redeem Lot's sin with his daughters? _____

5. What does that mean for you? _____

Sexual temptation will come. As with Joseph, our calling is to flee (Gen 38).

LESSON M-3

Pornography and Perversion

UNIT 2

OVERVIEW

Once we have established the biblical pattern for marriage, we have a kind of "zone defense" for addressing what's wrong with various perversions. For example, consider pornography: in the beginning, God made Adam and Eve, not Adam and a naughty picture, and this gives us the key to understanding the problems with pornography. What's missing from pornography is the other person, with all the parts that go with real personhood—hopes and dreams, likes and dislikes, needs and aspirations. Instead, that person is reduced to an object, a foil for someone's lust. Because marital sexuality is a God-given picture of Christ and the Church, a person indulging in pornography is lying about Christ's relationship to the Church, making an implicit claim that Christ exploits the Church for His own benefit without even knowing her, much less taking account of her needs. This twofold approach can be applied to any other perversion: (1) hold it up against the garden of Eden and and ask how it's different; and (2) hold it up against Christ and the Church and see whether the message it conveys is true.

SOURCE MATERIAL

- Ephesians 5:25-28
- 1 Corinthians 6:18

ACTIVITES

1. Shacking Up: What's Missing? Our culture tells us that not only is it okay to live with someone before you're married, but wise. What's wrong with shacking up (or living with someone before you're married) based on the picture given in Genesis?

What's missing in shacking up, based on the picture in Genesis? _____

_____

_____

How does living with someone before marriage lie about Christ and the Church? _____

_____

_____

Unit 2: Following Jesus the King

What kind of damage do you think those who shack up will have based on what's missing from their relationship? _____

_____

_____

_____

2. Journal Time: Flee Sexual Immorality. Spend some time writing in your journal or the space below about the following:

Confess any sexual sin you have committed. Don't forget to include lust; remember that Jesus equated lust with adultery. _____

_____

_____

_____

_____

Accept God's forgiveness for your sins. Accept the healing and wholeness Jesus gives because of His death on the cross. Write a prayer of acceptance in the space below. _____

_____

_____

_____

_____

Write out your commitment to flee from sexual immorality. If you struggle with something specific, address that struggle in your commitment. Ask God to strengthen you to stay away from sexual sin.

_____

_____

_____

_____

EVALUATION

1. What are the basic elements that Genesis teaches us need to be present in sexuality? _____
_____

2. How can we tell if some particular sexual practice is okay? _____
_____

3. When someone looks at pornography, what are they missing from the picture of marriage given in Genesis? _____
_____

4. What is the sinful engine that drives pornography and all other sexual perversions? _____
_____

5. According to Ephesians 5, what is marriage designed to be a picture of? _____
_____

6. How does viewing pornography lie about Christ? _____
_____

7. What does viewing pornography train the viewer to do? _____
_____

God created a beautiful garden full of animals and vegetation, and He put the man in it... but the woman was missing. This situation was "not good" (Gen 2:18). Masturbation removes the woman (or the man) from the picture. This is likewise "not good."

LESSON M-4

Masturbation and Making Out

UNIT 2

OVERVIEW

The previous lesson's approach applies in this lesson as well: take the topic back to the garden, and see what's missing. God did make Adam first, by himself, but then He looked at Adam (a solitary male) and said, "That's not good." The problem with masturbation is the same problem as with pornography: the other person is missing. The problem with making out is that although both people are present, God hasn't given them to each other yet. All that foreplay is designed to lead somewhere—we call it *fore*play for a reason—and they aren't yet able to go there. Making out before you're married is like getting on a plane to Boston and taking a parachute with you, planning to bail out over Ohio because you don't really want to go to Boston. Why get on the plane to start with?

SOURCE MATERIAL

- Genesis 1-2
- 1 Corinthians 7:3-5
- Song of Songs

ACTIVITES

1. What's Missing? (Again). Compare masturbation and making out to the garden of Eden. What's wrong with masturbation and making out based on the picture given in Genesis? _____

Masturbation

What's missing in masturbation, based on the picture in Genesis? _____
_____
_____

How does masturbation lie about Christ and the Church? _____
_____
_____

Unit 2: Following Jesus the King

What kind of damage do you think those who masturbate will have based on what's missing from their relationship?_____

_____

_____

Making Out

What's missing in making out, based on the picture in Genesis?_____

_____

_____

How does making out lie about Christ and the Church? _____

_____

_____

What kind of damage do you think those who make out will have based on what's missing from their relationship?_____

_____

_____

2. Journal Time: Making a Plan. It's all well and good to talk about not giving in to lust, not masturbating, etc., but in real life, the temptation can be overwhelming. Make a plan for what you will do when sexual temptation hits. If your plan includes nothing else, it should include prayer. Write out a simple prayer ahead of time.

My Plan:_____

_____

_____

_____

_____

_____

_____

Lesson M-4

EVALUATION

1. What are the basic elements that Genesis teaches us need to be present in sexuality? _____
_____
_____

2. How can we tell if some particular sexual practice is okay? _____
_____
_____

3. Why is masturbation deficient? What's wrong with it? _____
_____
_____

4. What are the problems with making out? _____
_____
_____

Jesus didn't condemn the woman caught in adultery, but He told her to "go and sin no more." We are called to have the same response with homosexuals (John 8:1-11).

LESSON M-5

Homosexuality

UNIT 2

OVERVIEW

We could have just handled homosexuality in Lesson M-3, but it's a hot-button issue in our culture, and it's worth taking a lesson to think it through. The departure from the biblical pattern is summed up in the old adage that in the beginning, "It was Adam and Eve, not Adam and Steve." But if it's so wrong, how come it feels so right for so many people? That is a good question, and the Bible gives us ways to think the answer to that question through. Sinful *acts* are moral choices for which we are responsible, but sinful *desires* are an innate part of being human after the fall. We are all broken in different ways: some of us are predisposed to drunkenness, others to anger, others to greed. It is not a strange thought for a Christian that a person might discover a predisposition to same-sex attraction. It is a very strange idea that it must be okay because someone has a predisposition toward it. It is not enough to try to love the sinner and hate the sin; we must hate the sin *because* we love the sinner and we understand that giving in to sinful predispositions damages him or her. As in every other human interaction, the Golden Rule applies: love your neighbor.

SOURCE MATERIAL

- Leviticus 18:22-30
- Leviticus 20:10-16
- John 8:1-12

ACTIVITES

1. Love Your Homosexual Friend. Imagine that you have found out that one of your friends is attracted to the same sex. What are some practical ways to show love to that person? Write some of your ideas below, and be prepared to discuss this question as a class.

2. Homosexual Marriage Ban. In small groups, discuss the following question.

A number of states have enacted state constitutional amendments specifically defining marriage as a union between a man and a woman, which effectively prevents the state from legalizing same-sex marriages. Would you vote in favor of such an amendment? Would you give your time and energy to help getting it passed (make phone calls, pass out fliers, ask people to sign petitions, etc.)? How would any of the following factors affect your answer?

- You have two unbelieving homosexual friends whom you are trying to win to Christ.
- You are billing the amendment as a "Defense of Marriage," but in your state, you could never pass a law calling for strict punishment on adultery—which would be a better defense of marriage. You realize that the amendment will pass only because a bunch of the people supporting it just hate homosexuals.
- You struggle with same-sex attraction yourself.

Lesson M-5

EVALUATION

1. How do we know that homosexuality is not part of God's design? _____
_____
_____

2. How does homosexuality fail to properly portray the image of God? _____
_____
_____

3. Why do homosexual unions not meet the biblical criteria for marriage? _____
_____
_____

4. "Homosexuality is a choice." Respond. _____
_____
_____

5. What makes a person attracted to the same sex? _____
_____
_____

6. Can homosexual desire be cured? _____
_____

7. How should we treat people caught up in homosexuality (or, for that matter, other sexual sins)? ___
_____
_____

Intimacy should always be protected by commitment. When there's more intimacy than commitment, it causes trouble.

LESSON M-6

Keeping Your Dignity

UNIT 2

OVERVIEW

We talked in Lesson M-2 about *why* to wait, but we haven't yet talked about *how* to wait. One of the single most important issues in waiting, for both men and women, is modesty. Modesty is about keeping your dignity—keeping intimacy at a level appropriate for the amount of commitment you have in the relationship. Understood in this way, modesty applies to emotions, not just necklines and hemlines. Modesty is also an area where good Christians can differ, and we need to handle the disagreements biblically.

SOURCE MATERIAL

- Proverbs 1:8-9, 7:10
- Song of Songs 2:7, 3:5, 8:4
- Romans 13:12-14:23

ACTIVITES

1. Reality Check. Imagine that you've met The One, and you're Going To Be Together Forever. Maybe Mom and Dad don't really understand, but that's okay—it's true love, and everything's going to work out. Now face and solve the real problems of taking care of each other on your own, just for a week.

How much money do you have *right now*? _____

_____

What ways do you have of earning more money? _____

_____

Where will you sleep each night for the next seven days? _____

_____

What will you eat for the next seven days? _____

_____

Unit 2: Following Jesus the King

What will you do about basic hygiene (showering, washing clothes, etc.)? _____

_____

If one of you gets sick enough to need a doctor, what will you do? _____

_____

2. Dress and Demeanor. Modesty is about demeanor as well as dress. Compare and contrast the two music videos below.

Shakira's "Hips Don't Lie" Music Video	Lindsey Stirling's Live Performance of "Electric Daisy Violin"

3. Learning the Language (Modesty Lab). Following the activity in class, answer the following questions.

What did you learn about modest dress? _____

_____

_____

Can a girl/woman dress modestly and still look attractive? _____

_____

_____

Lesson M-6

After participating in this activity, how will you think differently about how girls/women dress? Girls, are there any things you will change about the way you dress? _____
_____
_____

EVALUATION

1. What is the core issue with modesty? _____
_____
_____

2. What is emotional immodesty? _____
_____
_____

3. What are the underlying problems that produce emotional immodesty? _____
_____
_____
_____

4. What is physical immodesty? _____
_____
_____

5. What are the underlying problems that produce physical immodesty? _____
_____
_____

6. How can we learn to be emotionally and physically modest? _____
_____
_____

7. What do we do when we disagree about whether something is immodest or not? _____
_____

UNIT 3: FOLLOWING JESUS THE PROPHET

Prophets are all about speaking. Prophets withdraw into the desert to speak to God and hear His voice, then come out to call God's people and the world to repentance and belief in God. Throughout His earthly ministry, Jesus functioned as God's prophet. He often withdrew into the wilderness to pray, and when He spoke, He spoke with authority, not like the religious rulers of His day. He was able to speak with such authority because He heard God well, and that is the starting point for following Jesus the Prophet.

We learn to hear God speak first of all by reading Scripture well and then also by being receptive to God's guidance through His people. We are all united to Christ and therefore to one another, and God has given us the body of Christ as a resource and guide. With that understanding, we will then turn our attention to the different sorts of things that God often says: pronouncing blessing on us, calling us to confession and repentance, and comforting us. We will also take some time to see how God's people have approached God with their questions and how to respond in faith to what God reveals.

Being grounded in hearing God speak, we can then consider how to speak as God's representatives. If you are using the optional Devotional Apologetics Unit (Lessons 3.9-3.15), those lessons will build a foundation at this point for understanding unbelievers and learning to speak to them well and winsomely. (See the Introduction to Devotional Apologetics preceding Lesson 3.9 for more information.) Even without that unit, you will have sufficient foundation to address the question of whether it's arrogant to suppose that we have the truth and we can speak for God, and whether we have lives worth sharing with unbelievers.

The final lesson of the year is a recap of the signal responsibilities involved in following Christ as Priest, King, and Prophet. In that lesson, we pull together all we've learned and consider how it all operates synergistically in real life situations.

UNIT 3  FOLLOWING JESUS THE PROPHET

God miraculously knocked down the walls of Jericho (Josh 6). He always has and continues to do supernatural things.

LESSON 3.1

God Does Supernatural Things

UNIT 3

OVERVIEW

Talk to any Christian who's been around a while, and he can tell you tales of how God supernaturally intervened in his own life and in his friends' lives. People in biblical times had the same experience: throughout the Story, God is there and He intervenes. We should not be surprised when it happens to us, too.

SOURCE MATERIAL

- Unit summaries from the previous two years
- Psalms 78, 107

ACTIVITES

1. God Sightings in the Bible. Starting with creation and working all the way to the end of the Bible, write down as many supernatural events in the biblical Story as you can think of in the time your teacher gives you. Be prepared to discuss your answers with the class.

Unit 3: Following Jesus the Prophet

2. Contemporary God Sightings. In order to see how God continues to perform supernaturally, interview at least three Christians older than you. Ask them to tell you about any "God sightings"—moments when God supernaturally intervened in their lives. For the purposes of this activity, only firsthand accounts count; it has to be something that the interviewee personally experienced or witnessed. Write up your three stories and be prepared to share with the class. _____

_____
_____
_____
_____
_____
_____
_____

3. Psalm 107 Examples. Psalm 107 praises God for His works, but in a generic way that doesn't explicitly cite any historical events. Take each of the statements in the psalm and provide specific biblical examples of what God did. For example, verses 10-14 are exemplified in the Judges cycle. Some examples may apply more than once. _____

_____
_____
_____
_____
_____
_____
_____

Why do you think the psalmist wrote in such generic terms instead of giving specific examples like the psalmist did in Psalm 78? _____

_____
_____
_____

Lesson 3.1

EVALUATION

1. Name ten supernatural things God did in the biblical Story. _____

2. Does God still intervene supernaturally in the lives of His people today? _____

3. List three things that the author of Psalm 107 says God does. _____

4. Give an example of each of those three things from the biblical Story. _____

5. Give an example of each of those three things from the stories shared in class about God's supernatural acts today. _____

God's Word warns us of dangers we couldn't see for ourselves.

LESSON 3.2

Hearing God Through Scripture

UNIT 3

OVERVIEW

God has revealed Himself in the pages of Scripture. If we are seeking to know God's will and hear His voice, the Bible is the first place we should look.

SOURCE MATERIAL

- Genesis 3
- Psalm 19
- 2 Timothy 3:16-17

ACTIVITES

1. Psalm 19 Fleshed Out. Read Psalm 19:7-11.

What does David say the Scriptures do? _____
_____
_____
_____

Now, explain how the first five books of the Old Testament (which is all David had, remember) actually do what David says they can do. _____
_____
_____
_____
_____
_____
_____

Unit 3: Following Jesus the Prophet

2. Journal Time: Lectio Divina Lite. In Lesson 2.12, there was a chart of reading through the Psalms in a month. In your Bible, turn to the first Psalm for today's date. Either you, your teacher, or one of your classmates will read this Psalm out loud three times, and we will be seeking to hear God speak in the reading. After the reading, answer the following questions in your journal or the space below.

Write down any particular verse, statement or phrase that stuck out to you. Why do you think this verse or phrase stood out to you? _____
_____
_____
_____
_____
_____
_____
_____
_____

Consider the following questions about the item that stood out to you:

Is there something here that God wants me to know? _____
_____
_____
_____

Is there something here that God wants me to do? _____
_____
_____
_____

Is there something here that God wants me to stop doing? _____
_____
_____
_____

Lesson 3.2

EVALUATION

1. In Psalm 19, David lists a number of things that Scripture does. List three of them. _____
_____
_____
_____

2. What were the Scriptures that David was talking about at the time he wrote Psalm 19? _____
_____
_____

3. What are the four things Paul says Scripture is profitable for in 2 Timothy 3:16? List and define them. _____
_____
_____
_____
_____
_____
_____

4. If most of the Bible was not written directly *to* us, then why should we read those parts?_____
_____
_____
_____
_____
_____

God gave the Law to Moses on Mt. Sinai so Moses could give it to Israel (Exod 20). God speaks to us through other people even today.

LESSON 3.3

Hearing God Through His People

UNIT 3

OVERVIEW

Throughout the Bible God spoke to people directly, but many times He revealed and continues to reveal His will through the ministry of other people. We have been discussing the importance of reading the Bible well, but God even teaches us this skill through the ministry of His people. How to read the Bible well is far from the only thing God reveals to us through other people. Learning to recognize God's guidance through His people is an essential skill in the Christian life.

SOURCE MATERIAL

- 1 Corinthians 14:27
- Proverbs 11:14, 15:22
- Hebrews 13:7
- Ephesians 6:1-3

ACTIVITES

1. Authorities List. It can be difficult to figure out whom to ask for help on some issues, and it can be difficult sometimes to tell if we should follow their advice. But God has placed certain people of authority in our lives whom we must obey. Make a list of the authorities whom God has placed over you in different spheres of life. Include teachers, coaches, parents, church authorities, governmental authorities, and anyone else you can think of. _____

_____

_____

_____

_____

_____

_____

_____

Unit 3: Following Jesus the Prophet

2. Counselor List. Solomon says that there is safety in a multitude of counselors. Make a list below of people whom you might seek council from. _____

_____

_____

_____

_____

_____

_____

_____

_____

_____

After you have a list of advisors, go back through and answer the following questions: "Who would I ask for help with...

a broken friendship?"_____

a math problem?"_____

settling a fight with my brother/sister?"_____

what to do about an adult touching me inappropriately?"_____

_____

dealing with being jealous of my best friend?"_____

_____

my boy/girlfriend pressuring me to go further physically than I want to?"_____

_____

a teacher accusing me of cheating/plagiarism, when I didn't do it?"_____

_____

EVALUATION

1. If God has spoken to you, do you need to hear from anyone else? _____
_____
_____

2. How do we know that God wants Christians to listen to other Christians? _____
_____
_____

3. In one word, what is the key to the real life superpower of benefitting from advisors? _____
_____

4. What are the four key habits that contribute to benefitting from counsel?_____
_____
_____

5. How do you tell who would make a good advisor? _____
_____
_____
_____

6. There are counselors whose advice you can follow or not, and then there are authorities that you have to obey. Identify some authorities in your life._____
_____
_____
_____
_____

God has been speaking blessing to His people since He first blessed Adam and Eve in Genesis 1. Isaac followed God's example and blessed his sons (Gen 27).

LESSON 3.4

Hearing God Speak: Blessing

UNIT 3

OVERVIEW

People often fail to hear God because they expect Him to say certain things and don't recognize that He is speaking to them when He says something else. Scripture teaches us that God delights to bless His people.

SOURCE MATERIAL

- Genesis 1

ACTIVITES

1. A Brief History of Blessing. Work your way through the biblical Story, and write a list of all the ways in which God has blessed His people. Take your time.

Unit 3: Following Jesus the Prophet

2. Journal Time: Hearing Blessing. We have a God who is ready to bless His people. Often, we forget about His goodness and blessing. After your teacher's prayer, spend time writing in your journal or the space below whatever blessing the Lord brings to mind.

Lesson 3.4

EVALUATION

1. What is the first recorded thing God said to humanity? _____
_____

2. Did God continue to bless humanity? _____

3. List five occasions in the Bible when God blessed people. _____
_____
_____
_____
_____

4. Do you believe that God is willing to bless you today? _____
_____
_____

God promised that a seed of the woman would crush the head of the serpent (Gen 3:15).

LESSON 3.5

Hearing God Speak: Rebuke

UNIT 3

OVERVIEW

God is always eager to bless His children, but there are times when He does want to talk with us about our sin. When He addresses our sin, God moves toward us, always seeking a relationship with us, seeking to mend our understanding of Him so that we can partner with Him more effectively.

SOURCE MATERIAL

- Genesis 3
- *He Shall Crush His Head, Part 1,* Lessons 1.6-1.9
- Psalm 51

ACTIVITES

1. The Story of Rebuke. Beginning with God coming into the garden to seek out Adam and Eve after their sin, walk through the Story, looking at where God rebukes people and how He behaves when He does. Write as many examples as you can think of in the space below.

Unit 3: Following Jesus the Prophet

2. Journal Time: Confession Activity. Think back over the past day or so. Follow the directions below, writing your answers in your journal or the space below.

- Think back over the past day or so.
- Ask God to show you anything that He wants you to confess to Him. Wait and see what He will show you.
- Confess your sins to God. No excuses, no hiding, no renaming it to something less obnoxious. Confess it as it is.
- If you know them, confess the attitudes underlying your sin.
- Ask God to show you the truth. Don't assume that you know what He will say. Listen.
- Affirm the truth that God gives you. Say it out loud.

Lesson 3.5

EVALUATION

1. After Adam and Eve sinned, what did they do? _____
_____

2. Did Adam and Eve have to repent and seek God before He would talk with them? _____
_____

3. What did God do when He found Adam and Eve in the garden? _____
_____

4. When Adam and Eve had confessed their sin, what did God say first? _____
_____

5. What else did God say to Adam and Eve? _____
_____

6. What did God do about Adam and Eve's sin? _____
_____
_____
_____

7. What was Adam and Eve's purpose once God sent them out of the garden? _____
_____
_____

When Paul was shipwrecked, his companions panicked. But Paul heard comfort from God: no one would die. He spoke God's comfort to all those he was with (Acts 27:33-38).

LESSON 3.6

Hearing God Speak: Comfort

UNIT 3

OVERVIEW

Although most Christians expect to hear rebuke from God, many of us simply do not believe that God also speaks comfort to His people. But the Story shows us that God has been comforting His people from the very first sin onward, and He still speaks comfort to us today. Sometimes He changes the circumstances too, and sometimes He just changes us; but either way, He comforts us.

SOURCE MATERIAL

- Genesis 3
- Psalms 3, 13, 23
- Isaiah 36-37
- 1 Kings 19
- 2 Corinthians 12:7-10

ACTIVITES

1. Comfort in the Story. Work through the biblical Story, thinking of as many instances as you can where God comforted His people. As best as you can, write these examples of God's comfort on the timeline below, and be prepared to share your answers in class.

Unit 3: Following Jesus the Prophet

2. Journal Time: Seeking Comfort. Make a list of a few situations in your life that make you afraid, stressed or angry. _____

_____

_____

_____

_____

_____

Now, select the situation that bothers you the most and take it to God. Write out a prayer laying the whole problem before God. _____

_____

_____

_____

_____

_____

Once you've described the problem to God, ask Him to comfort you in whatever way would be best. If you want something in particular—a change in circumstances, a word of encouragement, or a change in your heart—that's okay. You should honestly tell God what you want. But you should also remain open to seeing what God wants to do. What did you hear from God?_____

_____

_____

_____

_____

_____

_____

_____

After you have written out your prayers, wait and see what God will do.

Lesson 3.6

EVALUATION

1. How did God comfort Adam and Eve in the garden? _____

2. How did God comfort Hezekiah? _____

3. How did God comfort Elijah? _____

4. How did God comfort Paul? _____

5. How can we seek comfort from God? _____

6. How do we sabotage ourselves when it comes to seeking comfort from God? _____

Job lost everything he had and initially responded well, never doubting God's goodness... but he forgot his place.

LESSON 3.7

Hearing God Speak: Questions and Answers

UNIT 3

OVERVIEW

We all have questions for God, but most Christians have never learned how to approach God well with their questions. Because we disregard the instruction and examples that Scripture gives, we get frustrated with God, and we never come to enjoy the conversational relationship with God that is our birthright. James gives us instruction, and Job and Habakkuk give us examples to learn from.

SOURCE MATERIAL

- Habakkuk
- Job
- James 1:5-8

ACTIVITES

1. Psalms Exploration. Come up with as many psalms as you can where the author is asking God tough questions about his situation like Habakkuk does at the beginning of his book. Try to start from memory, and only go to your Bible when you have run out of ideas. Come up with 15 psalms altogether and write them in the space below.

Unit 3: Following Jesus the Prophet

2. Asking God Questions. Make a list of the situations in your life that you find perplexing. The list can run the gamut from very personal ("Why didn't I make the basketball team?") to big and geopolitical ("What are we supposed to do with Christian Palestinian refugees?"). _____

_____
_____
_____
_____
_____
_____
_____
_____

Once you have the list, pick one question and spend some time praying about it each day for a week. Place a star next to this question in your list above. See what God will do when you pray faithfully. Try to remember to come back and write in your journal or the space below after your week of prayer is over. _____

_____
_____
_____
_____
_____
_____
_____
_____
_____

Lesson 3.7

EVALUATION

1. What did Job do right? _____
_____
_____
_____

2. What did Job do wrong? _____
_____
_____

3. What did Habakkuk do right? _____
_____
_____

4. What did Habakkuk do wrong? _____

5. What does James say we have to do to get wisdom from God? _____
_____

6. What does it mean to "ask in faith"? _____
_____
_____

7. What should we do if we can't ask in faith because we just don't trust God enough? _____
_____

Noah is a great example of faith. He built the ark before any floodwaters began to fall.

LESSON 3.8

Responding in Faith

UNIT 3

OVERVIEW

God loves to answer prayers for wisdom and guidance, but He isn't just answering us to satisfy our curiosity. He expects us to act on what He has shown us.

SOURCE MATERIAL

- Hebrews 11
- Joshua 1:8-9
- Proverbs 28:1

ACTIVITES

1. God's Word to Joshua. Look through the first few chapters of the book of Joshua and count all the times that someone tells Joshua to be courageous. Write the references below.

How many times is Joshua told to be courageous? _____

Who tells Joshua to be courageous? _____

Why do you think it happens so much? _____

Unit 3: Following Jesus the Prophet

2. Living Faith. This activity has several steps to it. Take your time and don't proceed to the next step until the previous one has been completed.

Begin with prayer. You might pray something like this, "Lord God, I know You built me to live the life You planned for me. Please guide me into a better understanding of that life now."

"Faith is the substance of things hoped for." What are the things that you hope for? What things, if you could actually do them, would bring you great joy? Make a list of those things. They can be big, goal-of-your-life things or little things; in fact, a good list will probably have both. And don't leave anything off the list just because it's impossible. _____

_____
_____
_____
_____
_____
_____
_____

Finished your list? Good. Let's move on to the next step. One of the things we have found is that a lot of the real work gets done when we push a little harder, go a little further beyond where we are comfortable stopping. So step two is to go back to your list and add three more things.

Take one of the items from your list that most resonates with you right now. This should be something that you would absolutely love to do—the dream of your heart (again, this can be big or small, a lifetime goal or something you want to do today). List out the steps that it would take to actually do it.

_____
_____
_____
_____
_____
_____

Now, ask yourself, "If that is the dream of my heart right now, then why am I not doing that? Why am I not taking those steps?" Write down your answers—all of them. Be brutally honest. Include your own character traits that stop you, the ways people treat you, the way the world works—any obstacle, anything that stands in your way.

Done with your list of obstacles? Good. Again, go back and add three more things to it.

Now, let's identify what we have. That list you just made? That is the enemy's blueprint for stopping you. Take all those things and lay them out before the Lord. You might pray something like this: "Father, it seems like You have put a desire in my heart for **(your dream here)** _____. At the same time, I honestly believe it can never happen because **(reason here)** _____. Please give me Your wisdom; tell me the truth about this." Wait and see what God will show you.

Let's go back to Hebrews 11:1. "Faith is the substance of things hoped for." Faith is the reality, the physical thing, the stuff right here, right now, of what you hope for. Faith is moving along the path, taking the steps—just like Abel making a sacrifice, Noah building a boat, Abraham packing up his stuff. So get out there and do it. Take the step—that's what faith is. So identify the first step toward the dream God has given you—and take it.

Unit 3: Following Jesus the Prophet

EVALUATION

1. What does the author of Hebrews say that faith is? _____
_____
_____

2. What does "the substance of things hoped for" mean? _____
_____
_____

3. What does "the evidence of things not seen" mean? _____
_____
_____

4. List some examples of faith given in Hebrews 11. _____
_____
_____

5. List some biblical examples of faith not mentioned in Hebrews 11. How did they demonstrate faith?
_____
_____
_____
_____

6. List some examples of faith from outside the Bible. How did they demonstrate faith? _____
_____
_____

The Apologetics House

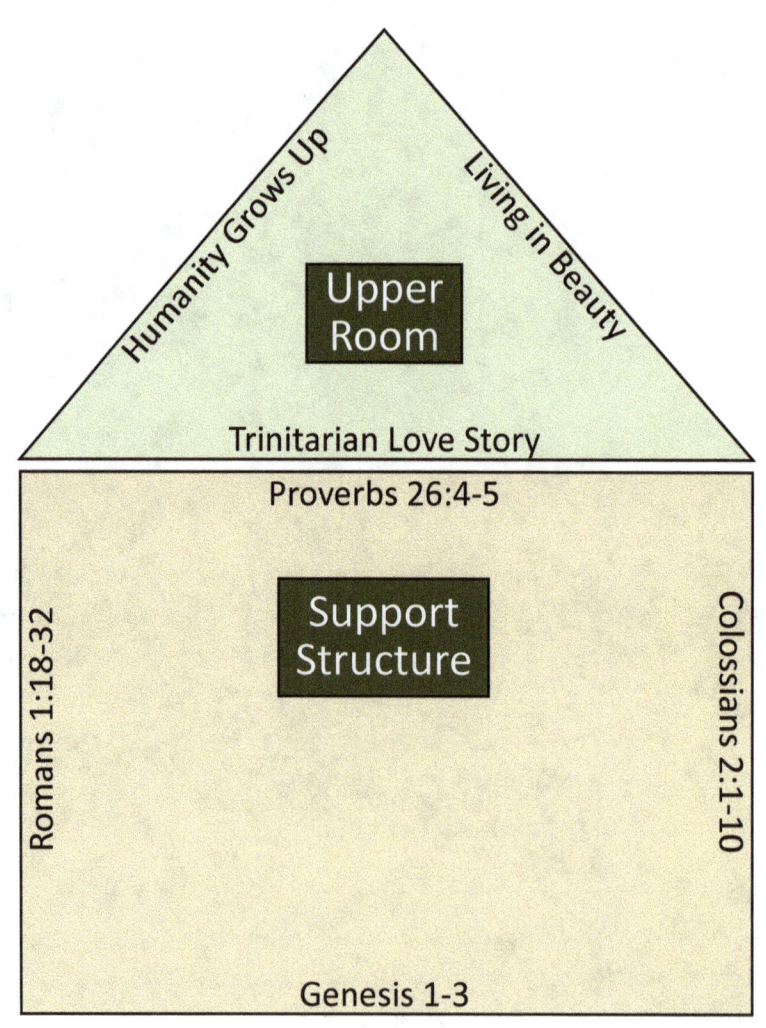

LESSON 3.9

Devotional Apologetics Lesson 1: Start with God's Word

UNIT 3

OVERVIEW

As with any other issue in Scripture, it is best in apologetics to begin at the beginning. By looking at the very beginning of human history with apologetics in mind, we learn about the key temptations that are at the very core of apologetics. These temptations are the same for believers and unbelievers, and we must learn to defeat them in our own hearts before we will be ready to address them in anyone else.

SOURCE MATERIAL

- Genesis 1-3
- Isaiah 55:10-11

ACTIVITES

1. Role Play. The point of this activity is to understand better the issue of ultimate authority. In pairs, or as a class against your teacher, argue whether Jesus ever lived.

- Unbelieving side: Your goal is to get your Christian discussion partner away from the Bible and arguing based on reason, science, evidence...anything but depending on God.
- Christian side: Your goal is to keep appealing to God and His Word. Never give up your ultimate authority. You are going to feel a little silly, and that's okay. Just don't make the Eve Mistake, and you'll be fine.

In the space below, write down some of the arguments you will use to support your position. _____
_____
_____
_____
_____
_____
_____

Unit 3: Following Jesus the Prophet

2. Journal Time. Write in your journal or the space below, considering the following:

How did you feel, sticking to the Scriptures in the face of an unbelieving challenge? Did you feel confident? Doubtful? Stupid? _____
_____
_____
_____
_____
_____
_____
_____

Can you imagine yourself doing the same thing with an actual unbeliever? Why or why not? _____
_____
_____
_____
_____

Take some time to pray and reflect on what you've learned in this lesson and how it applies to what you felt._____
_____
_____
_____
_____
_____
_____

Lesson 3.9

EVALUATION

1. What was Adam's Mistake?

2. What was Eve's Mistake?

3. Why is it impossible to be neutral toward God?

4. Can you use the Bible to win an argument with someone who doesn't believe the Bible? Why or why not?

5. If you use the Bible to prove Christianity, isn't that just circular reasoning? Explain.

When a Christian watches a beautiful sunset, he sees the glory of the God who created it. Not so for the unbeliever.

LESSON 3.10

Devotional Apologetics Lesson 2: Without Excuse

UNIT 3

OVERVIEW

Since we have a different ultimate authority than the unbeliever, how can we talk to him? What point of contact do we have? We have the world, and everything in it. God is always and everywhere confronting the unbeliever with the world, which points everyone to God. Once we understand that, we will be able to talk with the unbeliever about the world in a way that points back to God without making the Eve Mistake.

SOURCE MATERIAL

- Psalm 19
- Romans 1:18-32
- Psalm 14 by Sons of Korah (online video)

ACTIVITES

1. Thinking Through the Story. Throughout the biblical Story, there are many encounters between God's people and those who do not believe in Him. In the space below, make a list of as many of these encounters as you can think of and briefly write what happened at each encounter. _____

Unit 3: Following Jesus as Prophet

Throughout the Bible, how did God's people approach those who didn't believe in Him? _____
_____
_____
_____

How did the unbelievers respond? _____
_____
_____
_____

What can we learn from these past encounters? _____
_____
_____
_____

2. Journal Time: Reflecting on Psalm 14. After listening to the musical version of Psalm 14, write your thoughts about the psalm in your journal or the space below. You can use some of the following questions to help you.

What stood out to you about the psalm? _____
_____
_____
_____

How was listening to the psalm put to music different than simply reading the psalm? _____
_____
_____
_____

How does this psalm affect the way you think about unbelief? _____
_____
_____
_____

Lesson 3.10

EVALUATION

1. What biblical passage gives us an example of how to make a rational proof for God's existence? _____

2. According to the Bible, how does anyone know that God is there? _____

3. If everyone knows that God is there, then why are there so many atheists? _____

4. Why would anyone suppress the truth about God? _____

5. If we don't argue for God's existence based on the world, then what do we do? _____

6. How do we expose the emptiness of unbelief when it comes to cause and effect? _____

Adam and Eve failed because they forgot what God had said, distorting their reasoning and leading to sin. Everything worth having or knowing is hidden in Christ.

LESSON 3.11

Devotional Apologetics Lesson 3: Don't Get Robbed!

UNIT 3

OVERVIEW

An unbeliever necessarily denies the truth that he knows about God, but in reality he suppresses much more than just his knowledge of God. If the unbeliever is consistent with his unbelieving principles, it turns out that in fact he could know nothing at all. In Colossians 2, Paul teaches us that *all* the treasures of wisdom and knowledge are hidden in Christ. He also tells us that if we forget this truth, we get robbed.

SOURCE MATERIAL

- Colossians 2:1-10

ACTIVITIES

1. Apologetic Practice. Pair off with one of your classmates and take turns pretending to be an unbeliever. In the first round, let the believer challenge the unbeliever's basis for any kind of morality, and let the unbeliever defend it the best he can. In the second round, have the unbeliever challenge the believer with the problem of evil, and let the believer defend himself the best he can.

What did you learn?_____
_____
_____
_____
_____

Was it easy or hard to defend yourself as the believer? As the unbeliever?_____
_____
_____
_____
_____

Unit 3: Following Jesus as Prophet

2. Journal Time. Write in your journal or the space below about the following questions.

How do you feel about the claim that all the facts worth knowing and all the skills worth having are hidden in Christ? _____

_____
_____
_____
_____
_____

Why do you think Paul said that? _____

_____
_____
_____
_____

Do you think it's true?_____

_____
_____
_____
_____

How could you know if it's true or not? _____

_____
_____
_____
_____
_____

Lesson 3.11

EVALUATION

1. What does Colossians 2 say is hidden in Christ? _____
_____

2. What is a "treasure of wisdom"? Give three examples. _____
_____
_____
_____

3. What is a "treasure of knowledge"? Give three examples. _____
_____
_____
_____

4. What is the biblical basis for morality? _____
_____
_____
_____

5. Give two of the unbelieving theories for the basis of morality. _____
_____
_____
_____

6. Why do the unbelieving theories for morality fail? _____
_____
_____
_____

The rebels had to build the tower of Babel out of God's earth; they couldn't make their own. Everything people build to avoid dealing with God is built with what God gave them, and founded in the world He made.

LESSON 3.12

Devotional Apologetics Lesson 4: Answer a Fool

UNIT 3

OVERVIEW

It's one thing to know that the unbeliever's position is self-defeating, but it's another thing entirely to find the weaknesses and expose them so that the unbeliever can see the weaknesses—and do all that without sinking to the unbeliever's level at the same time. In this lesson, we learn the biblical standards for interacting with unbelief and observe some examples of people who do it well.

SOURCE MATERIAL

- Proverbs 26:4-5

ACTIVITES

1. Collision. After watching the film *Collision*, answer the following questions, and be prepared to discuss your answers.

Describe Doug Wilson's demeanor and attitude throughout the movie. What was his relationship with Christopher Hitchens like? _____

_____

_____

What question did Wilson ask over and over? _____

_____

_____

_____

Where did you see foolishness in Hitchens' presentation? _____

_____

_____

_____

_____

Unit 3: Following Jesus as Prophet

2. Bahnsen-Stein Debate. After listening to or reading the debate, answer the following questions and be prepared to discuss your answers.

What is Bahnsen's core argument? What is Stein's? _____
_____
_____
_____
_____

Do you think Bahnsen's argument works? What about Stein's? _____
_____
_____
_____

Why do you think Bahnsen didn't argue along the lines Stein was expecting? _____
_____
_____
_____

Did Stein respond to Bahnsen's argument? _____
_____
_____
_____

Do you think it was possible for Stein to respond to Bahnsen's argument? How? _____
_____
_____
_____

Where did you see foolishness in Stein's argumentation? _____
_____
_____
_____

Lesson 3.12

EVALUATION

1. What is the biblical standard for interacting with a fool? _____
_____
_____

2. What does "answer a fool according to his folly" mean? _____
_____
_____

3. What does "do not answer a fool according to his folly" mean? _____
_____

4. Why are we referring to the unbeliever as a fool? Isn't that rude? _____
_____
_____

5. Should we call the unbeliever a fool when we're talking to him? _____
_____
_____

When Adam and Eve sinned, they broke the world and were sent out from the garden. But God sent His Son to bring hope and healing. We are called to participate in His victory in this broken world by loving others.

LESSON 3.13

Devotional Apologetics Lesson 5: Loving the Different

UNIT 3

OVERVIEW

God made a world where we have the privilege to be His self-portrait by living loving lives. When we love each other, and especially when we love people who are unlovely or who hate us, we are the image of God. You may never argue an unbeliever into feeling the foolishness of his unbelief, but any Christian can love, and love shows up the foolishness of unbelief as nothing else can.

SOURCE MATERIAL

- Genesis 1-2
- John 14-17
- 1 John

ACTIVITES

1. Telling the Story. Your challenge is to tell the biblical Story as a love story between God and humanity, as your teacher modeled in class. Starting at the beginning, write down as many "episodes" of the Story as you can and how each is part of a love story. Be prepared to share with the class.

Unit 3: Following Jesus as Prophet

Lesson 3.13

2. Journal Time: A Week in the Upper Room. Every day for the next week, read the Upper Room Discourse (John 14-17). Each day, make a note of one thing from the reading that caught your attention.

Day 1:_____
_____
_____

Day 2:_____
_____
_____

Day 3:_____
_____
_____

Day 4:_____
_____
_____

Day 5:_____
_____
_____

Day 6:_____
_____
_____

Day 7:_____
_____
_____

At the end of the week, look back over your comments and think about your behavior this past week. Overall, what stands out to you the most about the Upper Room Discourse?_____
_____(continued on next page)

Unit 3: Following Jesus as Prophet

Did your time reading this passage change your behavior in any way? _____
_____
_____
_____
_____

3. Loving in Deed and in Truth. "My little children, let us not love in word and in tongue, but in deed and in truth" (1 John 3:18). List three concrete ways you can image the love of God by doing something definite. Each item should have a definite time boundary—today, tomorrow, this weekend—but at least one should be something you can do today. _____

Lesson 3.13

EVALUATION

1. Can you think of anyone who was ever argued into becoming a Christian? _____
_____
_____
_____

2. How do you think most people become Christians? _____
_____
_____
_____

3. In the Upper Room Discourse, what does Jesus say will convert the world? What do you think it will take for that to happen? _____
_____
_____
_____

4. Other than the ways mentioned already in the lesson, name three episodes in the Story that you could use to talk about how much God loves humanity. _____
_____
_____
_____

5. Name three examples of ways that you can live a more loving life. Be specific. _____
_____
_____
_____
_____
_____

Violence entered the world very early—the first son of Adam and Eve killed the second. But, we have matured, and in places around the world where Christianity has had a long-term impact, violence is quite uncommon.

LESSON 3.14

Devotional Apologetics Lesson 6: Growing to Maturity

UNIT 3

OVERVIEW

Many unbelievers long to see the day that humanity grows up enough to make wise decisions. Different people have different issues that they care about—war, hunger, poverty, business, the environment, family life and so on—but most people care about something and believe that we're messing it up badly. Christianity tells an optimistic story of the world, a story in which humanity really does grow up into maturity, and the world is saved through Jesus Christ.

SOURCE MATERIAL

- Matthew 13:33
- Psalm 2
- Acts 4:23-31
- Revelation 20-21

ACTIVITES

1. Remember the Ending. Bring in a news article that reports some pretty serious bad news and be prepared to briefly summarize your article to the class. Following your class discussion, write a prayer in your journal or the space below, thanking Him for the good ending we have in Christ.

Unit 3: Following Jesus as Prophet

2. Journal Time: Do You Believe It? Write in your journal or the space below on the following questions.

Do you really believe that every last one of the problems that now afflict the world will be resolved in the end? Every rape, kidnapping and murder will be set right, every environmental problem will be solved, every tyranny will be dissolved, every injustice dealt with? Do you have a hard time believing any of that?_____
_____
_____

Do you really believe that all will be well in the end? Why or why not?_____
_____
_____
_____
_____

Whatever things you're having trouble believing that God can resolve—take those things before God in prayer. Be honest with God about your doubts and ask Him to tell you what He wants you to know about theses things. You may use the space below to write your prayer._____
_____
_____
_____
_____
_____
_____
_____
_____
_____
_____

Lesson 3.14

EVALUATION

1. The understanding of history that was presented in this lesson—that things are slowly improving through the gospel over time—does that surprise you? Why or why not? _____
_____
_____

2. How violent was the pre-flood world, compared to our society? Give an example. _____
_____
_____

3. How violent was the world Jesus was born into, compared to our society? Give an example. _____
_____
_____
_____

4. Why is our society less violent? _____
_____

5. Name a way that a king a thousand years ago was poorer than most poor people in America today.
_____
_____
_____
_____
_____

6. Why did the apostles pray Psalm 2 when they were threatened and told not to preach Jesus? _____
_____
_____
_____
_____

Peter and John healed a lame man in the name of Jesus; their lives were enriched by Jesus and they passed this richness on (Acts 3).

LESSON 3.15

Devotional Apologetics Lesson 7: Living in Beauty

UNIT 3

OVERVIEW

Being able to argue well is a valuable skill, and being able to tell the Christian Story well is an even more valuable skill. But when it comes to winning people to Christ, most people are far more persuaded by how Christians live than by what Christians say. Living beautifully is the best apologetic we can have.

SOURCE MATERIAL

- Matthew 10
- 2 Corinthians 4, 11

ACTIVITES

1. Self-Evaluation. Look over the list of questions below. Don't try to answer them all, just pick one that really jumps out at you.

- How do I handle it when I don't get my way?
- Do I get jealous when someone has more (money, popularity, talent, good looks, better grades, etc.) than I do?
- How often am I really at peace?
- What does it take to make me happy? Unhappy?
- What do I do about it when I'm unhappy?
- When was the last time I was really grateful for something?
- When my friends are happy/sad, can I be happy/sad with them?
- Does anybody else want the kind of relationship I have with (God, friends, parents, siblings, teachers, coaches, etc.)?
- Do I praise God no matter what's happening?
- What's so great about being a Christian right now?

Spend some time answering the question in your journal or the space on the following page.

Unit 3: Following Jesus as Prophet

2. Prayer Activity. Read 2 Corinthians 11:24-28. This was Paul's life. Everywhere he went, people wanted to kill him. But everywhere he went, people wanted to be like him—they wanted what he had, and they came to Christ so they could have it too. With that in mind, think about the following questions and write some notes in the space provided.

Who would want my life? Do I have a life that an unbeliever would want? _____

Is there a part of my life I could invite an unbelieving friend into? _____

If so, how could I share that part of my life with an unbelieving friend? (Not brag about it, but actually share it with them.) _____
_____
_____
_____

What parts of my life are no different from an unbeliever's? Make a list. _____
_____
_____
_____
_____
_____
_____

Ask God, "Which area of my life do You want me to focus on right now?" _____
_____
_____
_____
_____
_____

Ask God, "What do You want this area of my life to look like? And how do I get there?" _____
_____
_____
_____
_____
_____

Many in Ephesus found that the way of Jesus was better than their sorcery, and they burned their books of magic.

LESSON 3.16

Is It Arrogant To Think We Have The Truth?

UNIT 3

OVERVIEW

Isn't it arrogant to think that you alone have the truth, and everybody else is just wrong? On the other hand, isn't it equally arrogant to assume that nobody can know the truth, or that it doesn't matter what the truth might be? We got here somehow, and people really do believe something about that. So the question is, how can we come to know?

SOURCE MATERIAL

- Acts 17:16-34
- Matthew 13:3-8

ACTIVITES

1. Old Testament Background. Read through Paul's speech on Mars' Hill (Acts 17:22-31). Then, for each of the references below, write down which part of the Old and New Testament Story Paul was referring to. Feel free to add additional references if you would like.

Acts 17:24:_____

_____

_____

Acts 17:25:_____

_____

_____

Acts 17:26:_____

_____

_____

Acts 17:31:_____

_____

_____

Unit 3: Following Jesus the Prophet

Which parts of the Story was Paul choosing to tell the Athenians, and why did he choose those particular parts? _____
_____
_____
_____
_____
_____

2. Finding the Altar to the Unknown God. Paul found a point of contact within the Athenian culture that would give him a way to speak to the Athenians. Your challenge is to find the points of contact that will allow you to proclaim the message of Jesus. Look what Paul did: he found a place where the culture knew itself to be lacking, and he used that to open a door. What is it that your friends don't know how to understand? Where are the gaps in their lives where they don't know what to do? Where has God done something in your friend's life, and he doesn't realize it's God? Here are some things to look for:

- Blessings that God has given your friend
- Situations where your friend is distressed and doesn't know what to do
- Places where our culture acknowledges God, sometimes without really meaning to

Write as many points of contact you can think of in the space below and be prepared to discuss your answer with the class. _____
_____
_____
_____
_____
_____
_____
_____
_____
_____

Lesson 3.16

EVALUATION

1. What was the altar to the unknown god? How did it come to be in Athens? _____
_____
_____
_____
_____

2. Why did Paul choose that altar as his point of contact? _____
_____
_____
_____
_____

3. What parts of the biblical Story did Paul tell? Why? _____
_____
_____
_____
_____

4. How did Paul respond when the philosophers insulted him? _____
_____
_____
_____
_____

5. Is there a way to present the truth without sounding arrogant? _____
_____
_____
_____
_____

God wants to invite the entire world into His kind of life. Jesus modeled this by feeding the 5,000. We are called to show the world what life can really be like in Christ and invite them into it.

LESSON 3.17

A Life Worth Sharing

UNIT 3

OVERVIEW

"Freely you have received; freely give" (Matt 10:8). God tells us: I give different things to each of you. I'm not asking you to do or be the same things as everyone else. I am telling you to take whatever it is that I have given you and share it. Do it for Me, because I delight in it. Share with My people, for their benefit and growth. Give your talents to the world, because I love them. When you walk with Me, you will always have a life worth sharing.

SOURCE MATERIAL

- Matthew 10:1-8
- Psalm 139

ACTIVITES

1. Helping People Dream. Brainstorm some questions you can ask people to help them start to reconnect to their dreams. You can start with the questions your teacher gave as examples in this lesson. Then add your own questions. What other questions could you ask that would get at the same things from a slightly different angle? Be prepared to discuss your answer with the class.

Unit 3: Following Jesus the Prophet

2. Faith You Can Share. The activity below is similar to the Living Faith activity in Lesson 3.8. If you didn't do that activity, go back and do it. Then, walk another person (a friend or even a stranger) through the activity below. Just share it! If it's appropriate, you can write down their responses in the spaces provided while you talk with them. It very well may not be appropriate, especially if you are talking with a stranger. Use your judgment.

If you could do anything, anything at all, what would you do? Say that somehow you knew, for sure, that the money and everything else would get taken care of, and you really could do anything you wanted, what would you do? _____

_____

_____

_____

_____

_____

What would it take to achieve that dream? List anything you can think of that would move you closer to the dream. Don't worry about whether any of these steps are possible or not, just make a list of everything you can think of. _____

_____

_____

_____

_____

_____

What are the obstacles? Why aren't you doing it right now? What are all the reasons that this dream is never going to happen? _____

_____

_____

Go back and add three more things to both lists. Yeah, I know, you've already listed everything you can think of. Do it anyway.

Now, interpret the lists.

The first list is what faith looks like in your life.

The second list is the enemy's strategy. That's how he's going to stop you from being the person God made you to be, from stepping into the destiny that God planned for you.

Let's tackle the second list, using what we know about confession and repentance. Confession is telling God where you're at. So confess the second list to Him: "God, I don't believe that_____ _____ **(your dream here)** can ever happen, because _____ **(your obstacle here)**. I believe this obstacle is so big, even You can't overcome it. Please speak to me and tell me what's true." Then listen, and see what God says to you. Write any of your thoughts or God's words to you below._____

"Faith is the substance of things hoped for." So get out your first list and ask God which one of those steps He wants you to tackle. Then ask Him how to go about tackling that step. Listen and do what He shows you. Write what He says to you below._____

Unit 3: Following Jesus the Prophet

3. Freely You Have Received. Read Matthew 10:1-8. These disciples had been with Jesus and had seen Him heal the sick, cast out demons, and preach the gospel. He gave them the power to go and do the same, and said, "Freely you have received, freely give." Make a list of things you have received from God. List the gifts, skills and talents God has given you, the times God has comforted you, the wisdom God has shared with you, the material things He has blessed you with—anything you can think of—in the space below._____

_____

_____

_____

_____

_____

_____

_____

_____

Now, write down some ways you could share those things with others, and put the things you write down into practice!_____

_____

_____

_____

_____

_____

_____

_____

EVALUATION

1. Why do you believe that each person has a unique identity? _____
_____
_____

2. Why do you believe that each person has a unique destiny? _____
_____
_____

3. List three questions that can help to access someone's hopes and dreams. _____
_____
_____

4. True or False: The most important thing about living by God's rules is meeting all the moral requirements like not stealing or committing adultery. Explain._____
_____
_____
_____

5. List five things that God has given you, and give at least one way you can apply "Freely you have received; freely give" to each of them._____
_____
_____
_____
_____

The Triple-Triangle: Following Jesus as Priest, King and Prophet

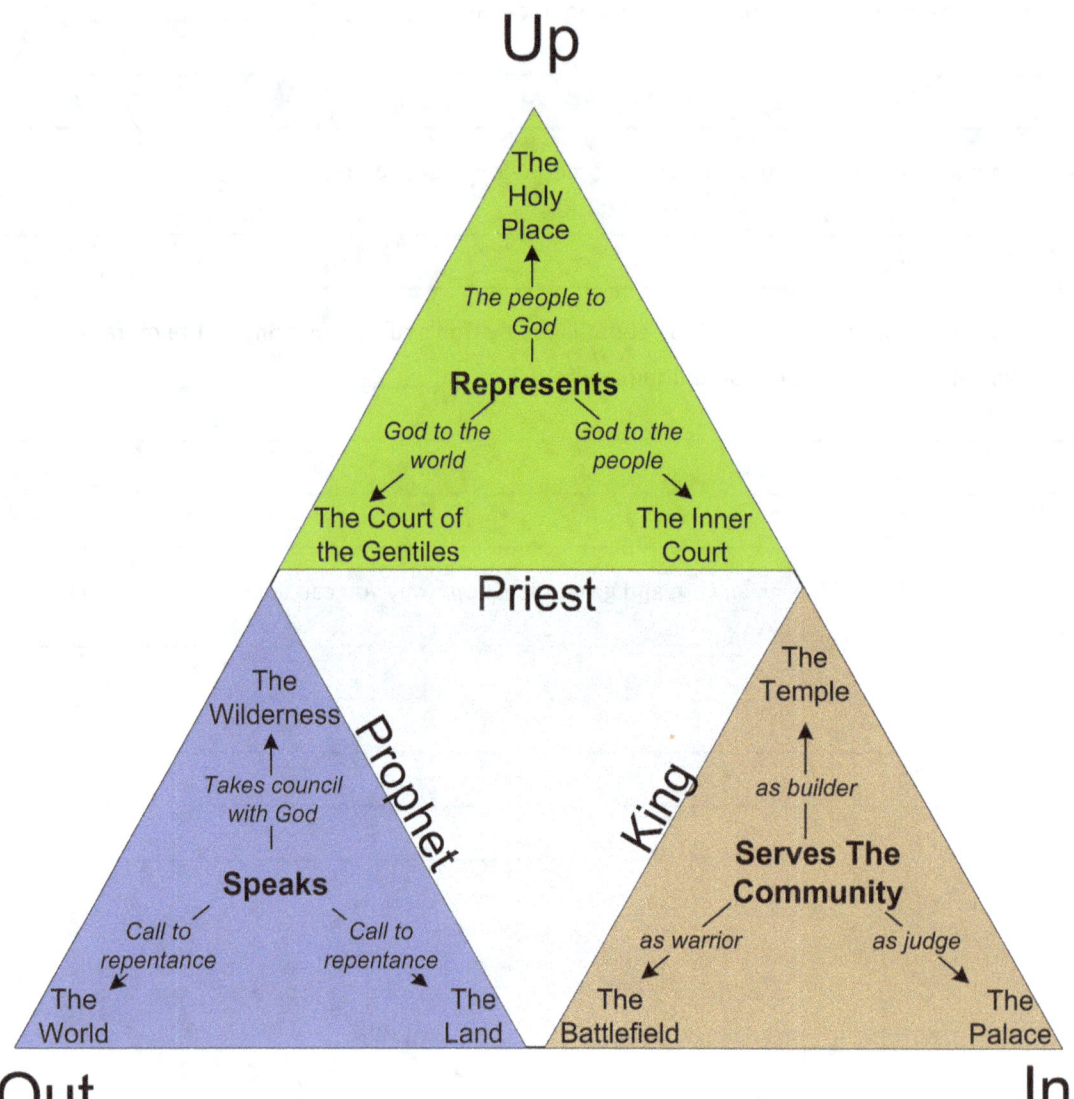

LESSON 3.18

The Triple-Triangle: Following Jesus as Priest, King and Prophet

UNIT 3

OVERVIEW

Throughout the Old Testament Story, we learn how priests, kings and prophets each have their own responsibilities and behave in different ways. In Jesus, those three roles are brought together in one Person—and He is the Person we are called to follow.

SOURCE MATERIAL

- Genesis 14:17-20
- Exodus 19 and 24
- 1 Samuel 1, 12, and 17
- 2 Samuel 6
- 1 Kings 3 and 19
- 2 Kings 23
- Daniel 2

ACTIVITES

1. Three Options. For each of the following situations, identify whether it is an up, in, or out situation. Then write how you could respond to the situation as a priest, as a king and as a prophet. How would those three responses differ from each other?

Planned Parenthood wants to build a clinic in your town.

Up, in, or out?_____
_____

Response as a priest:_____
_____
_____

Response as a king:_____
_____

Unit 3: Following Jesus the Prophet

Response as a prophet:_____
_____
_____

Which response would you prefer?_____
_____

One of your friends finds out she's pregnant. She doesn't know what to do; there's no way she's ready to have a child. She's considering abortion.

Up, in, or out?_____
_____

Response as a priest:_____
_____
_____

Response as a king:_____
_____
_____

Response as a prophet:_____
_____
_____

Which response would you prefer?_____
_____

Some families in your church have been feeding homeless people at a local park every Wednesday for the past year. Last week, the police showed up and ticketed your friends for publicly serving food without a permit. (This actually happened in Daytona Beach, FL.)

Up, in, or out?_____
_____

Response as a priest:_____
_____

Lesson 3.18

Response as a king: _____
_____
_____

Response as a prophet: _____
_____
_____

Which response would you prefer? _____
_____

<u>Same scenario as above…but it's two months later. Your friends have tried to get a permit, and the city won't give them one.</u>

Up, in, or out? _____
_____

Response as a priest: _____
_____
_____

Response as a king: _____
_____
_____

Response as a prophet: _____
_____
_____

Which response would you prefer? _____
_____

<u>One of your friends tells you he or she is gay.</u>

Up, in, or out? _____
_____

Response as a priest: _____

Unit 3: Following Jesus the Prophet

_____

Response as a king:_____

_____

Response as a prophet:_____

_____

Which response would you prefer?_____

2. Journal Time: What's Your Preference? Take some time to consider whether you prefer to respond in priestly, kingly or prophetic ways.

Part 1. Write out some examples of common or recent situations where you have responded in your preferred way. _____

_____
_____
_____
_____
_____
_____
_____

Part 2. For each of those situations you listed, consider responses from the other two categories. For example, if you naturally default to a King response, try to come up with good Priest and Prophet responses to the same situation._____

_____
_____
_____
_____
_____
_____
_____

Part 3. Share some of these real life situations and the responses you have come up with.

EVALUATION

1. What is the primary responsibility of a priest? _____

2. What is the primary responsibility of a king? _____

3. What is the primary responsibility of a prophet? _____

4. Draw the triple-triangle and fill it in. Include the upward, inward and outward responsibilities of Priest, King and Prophet. For bonus points, include the places where these responsibilities take place.

5. Give an example from the Story for each of the points on the triple-triangle (i.e., an up, in and out example for each of the three roles—nine examples in all). _____
_____
_____
_____

6. Give some Old Testament examples where the Priest, King and Prophet responsibilities overlapped.
_____
_____
_____

END OF YEAR ACTIVITIES

1. **Telling the Story.** You have spent three years now working with the biblical Story. Write out the Story from end to end, working from the photo mosaic at the beginning of the workbook, and touching on every picture.

2. **Telling the Story Thematically.** Choose a theme that you like, and recount the Story in terms of your chosen theme. You don't have to use every picture, but you need to recount the entire Story as a single, coherent story.

3. **Shoebox Diorama.** Break up into small groups of three and come up with a plan to represent the entire biblical Story in a shoebox diorama. Then write up a paragraph description of your proposed diorama to share with the class (with illustrations, if you like).

www.ingramcontent.com/pod-product-compliance
Lightning Source LLC
Chambersburg PA
CBHW081138010526
44110CB00061B/2509